"With clarity and efficiency Andre rips ... d shines such brilliant light upon them that ... ir excitement. I guarantee you that all throug... ... will be saying "Wow, I've read that scripture so many times before but have never understood it like this!"

[Ryan Rufus - Pastor, *City Church International*, Hong Kong (ccihk.com); Founder, *New Nature Publications* (www.newnaturepublications.com); Author of *Sanctification by Grace* and *Do Christians Still Have a Sinful Nature?*]

"What a treat to read a truly non-religious book that effectively reveals God's amazing grace towards mankind. In this book Andre clearly shares Jesus; who he is, what he's done and what life in him is all about. Explained is the huge difference between Old and New Covenant living and the common problem of mixture. Reading this book could cause you to experience new found identity, freedom, and boldness."

[Art Henkel - Director, *Grace Connection Canada* (www.graceconnection canada. com)]

"Over the past few years I have found Andre's writings to be very helpful in unpacking the gospel of grace. You might be surprised to learn, as I was, that he was once a modern day Pharisee (his words, not mine). I find it fascinating that often the best teachings on grace come from those who once vehemently opposed it. Andre is in good company and this is a good book! It is more than a collection of topical writings. It's a record of a journey from performance-oriented religion to liberating, life-giving grace. I highly recommend it."

[Paul Ellis (escapetoreality.org), New Zealand]

"This is one of the most courageous and convincingly clear books on the beauty of God's acceptance Grace and freedom from condemnation. It is a brilliant and well researched biblical reply to the angry Pharisees' festering indignation at the spreading happiness caused by the Grace revolution. If anyone has tried to steal your joy and freedom in Christ this book will fully reassure you and release you into the Glorious liberty that God intended for His sons and daughters. Well done Andre."

[Rob Rufus - Pioneer of Grace and Pastor, *City Church International*, Hong Kong (ccihk.com); Author of *The Grace of God* and *Invading the Impossible*]

"Andre's book systematically reveals God's Grace in practical and easy to understand ways. Whether you are new to grace or not, the principles in this book will help you to better grasp the depths of the goodness and love of our Father. Read it slowly, you won't want to miss a thing!"

[Cornel Marais - Founder of Charisma Ministries: Making the Supernatural NATURAL (www.charismaministries.org); Author of *So You Think Your Mind Is Renewed?*]

"This is more than a few personal opinions on grace. This book stands as an excellent concise commentary on the subject that breaks misconceptions, stirs faith, builds confidence and refutes the cynical critics. There is grace reformation sweeping the earth and Andre has done much to further its advance. A recommended and essential resource for all grace exponents."

[Tony Ide - Pastor, *Freedom Life Fellowship*, Perth, Australia (www.freedomlife. org.au)]

"I like books that challenge the way people think. Books that cause the reader to go back and reevaluate some of the things that they've always believed and ask themselves if those viewpoints are biblical or simply a result of what they've been taught by somebody else. *Grace, the Forbidden Gospel* is such a book. It is a book that will stimulate your mind and refresh your heart.

Andre van der Merwe has taken the reader back to the drawing board of Scripture in a way will help set people free from the faulty views of God, themselves, others and life in general. This book will make you stop and think. You may not agree with everything the author sets forth, but you will be forced to take another look at the biblical reason you embrace the position your currently hold. Upon taking that second look, you might find yourself moving into a new, grace-based understanding of some things you've thought you already had a clear grasp on up until now.

The climate of the church of Jesus Christ today finds itself in a place where legalism has a debilitating effect on many people. Across the world, the focus within the church is largely on our behavior and how we need to do a better job in living the Christian life if we expect God to move on our behalf and in our midst. The result of that focus has been devastating. The only antidote to this problem is grace and that's what this book is all about.

I predict that *Grace, the Forbidden Gospel* will set many free from that paradigm and bring them into the place of grace. Most Christians today are tired of the worn out religious treadmill they've spent most of their lives performing on and are ready for the message of grace. As you read these pages, you may find yourself feeling the refreshing breeze of Agape, inviting you to give up any notion that the level of victory you experience in your spiritual walk is up to you and to simply rest in the One who has already accomplished it all on behalf of all of us.

Read this book slowly and prayerfully. Keep your Bible handy to compare what the author says with what the Scripture says. In doing this, you will likely find yourself experiencing a sense of freedom and joy that can only be known by those who are willing to rise above the programming we may have received through legalistic, albeit sincere, influences of our past. As we rise above those legalistic influences, we will begin to see the Light of Grace in a way that will have a permanent transformational effect on our lives."

[Steve McVey - President, *Grace Walk Ministries* (www.gracewalk.org); Author of *Grace Walk, Grace Rules, Grace Amazing, A Divine Invitation, The Godward Gaze, The Grace Walk Experience and Walking in The Will of God*]

GRACE, the Forbidden Gospel

Jesus tore the veil. Religion sewed it back up.

Andre van der Merwe

WestBow

PRESS

A DIVISION OF THOMAS NELSON

WestBow Press books may be ordered through booksellers or by contacting:

WestBow Press
A Division of Thomas Nelson
1663 Liberty Drive
Bloomington, IN 47403
www.westbowpress.com
1-(866) 928-1240

ISBN: 978-1-4497-1403-1 (sc)
ISBN: 978-1-4497-1404-8 (hbk)
ISBN: 978-1-4497-1402-4 (e)

Library of Congress Control Number: 2011924215

Printed in the United States of America

WestBow Press rev. date: 5/4/2011

Contents

Introduction

You might want to burn this book after reading the first chapter. Then again, you might devour it in a few days...

If you've never been exposed to hearing the gospel preached by Paul the Apostle in its pure, undiluted form, this book might offend and possibly even anger you. The gospel of grace has been outlawed and frowned upon by most organized religious institutions. Take courage though, there is a generation of believers rising up in the earth whose eyes are opening to the truth of the gospel of grace – a wave of people that has grown fed up with the way that church is done: Either good news is preached with some guilt and manipulation mixed in, or church services take the form of well orchestrated shows. Many believers' entire lives are reduced to nothing more than a sin management program, running the endless treadmill of trying to please God by doing more for Him or trying to sin less.

If you have been raised with religion, then understanding the gospel of grace may involve unlearning most of what you have learnt through the years. It may initially feel as though the carpet is being plucked from under your feet, but as the perfume of God's love rises and the truth of the Word begins to set you free, you will find yourself unable to resist the Father's romantic advances, drawing you into Himself for a deeper experience of who He is.

The gospel of grace (that was first given to Paul in a revelation from God - Gal 1:12) shook the foundations of the religious world of his day. Paul preached a different message than Jesus, but for a good reason: They were living under different covenants. Jesus condemned the religious Pharisees and Scribes for trying to uphold their own "watered down" version of the law, but He showed compassion to sinners. Paul understood that Christ was the fulfillment of the law and he preached God's love and acceptance *apart* from trying to uphold the law's requirements. Both were however persecuted for their message by the religious leaders of their day. This is why "religion" is rightfully considered today by many (especially non-believers) as one of the most destructive forces on the planet.

"Religion" is a powerless form of godliness that robs people of a real relationship with their Maker and drives them into a lifestyle of endless frustration and doubt about whether they are ever *really* saved. All of that can change by reading this book.

Difficult Questions in the Bible

Have you ever been stuck with some of those theological questions that simply would not go away? Have you ever wondered why it feels as though there is something "missing" at church? Have you ever considered why you never seem to have boldness when you pray, with that niggling feeling of guilt and unworthiness always in the back of your mind? This book will help you to:

- Discover the golden thread of God's love that runs through the Bible, starting with Adam and Eve in the Garden of Eden, understanding why it appears as though He "changed His mind" in the Old Testament (severely punishing Israel and allowing thousands of people to be massacred) and how this picture of God has warped and influenced our view of Him.

- Find out why there is famine and wars and hurt in the world today when God claims to be a loving God.

- Be swept along in this journey of clearing away the fog surrounding those seemingly harsh and contradictory verses in the Bible.

- Understand what happens to the spirit, soul and body of a believer the moment they are born again.

- Disarm those "intimidating" verses and perceptions that always seem to put you on the back foot, such as the unforgivable sin, tithing, Job's afflictions, the 10 Commandments, etc.

- And many more.

If you find yourself angered and offended by the first few chapters, simply press on regardless - the answers will come.

> *So shall My word be that goes forth from My mouth; it shall not return to Me void, but it shall accomplish what I please, and it shall prosper in the thing for which I sent it. (Isa 55:11 NKJV)*

Mission Statement

Once again in the church there is a struggle for a theological reformation that will liberate believers to break free from the yoke of bondage that has been put on the children of God by people who may have had good intentions, but that have only taught the religious doctrines and traditions that they themselves have been taught.

The written code of the law was cancelled over 2000 years ago at the cross.

> *Having wiped out the handwriting of requirements that was against us, which was contrary to us. And He has taken it out of the way, having nailed it to the cross. (Col 2:11 NKJV)*

Yet it is still widely preached and believed that we have to measure up to some standard or try to relate to God through our level of obedience. The entire New Covenant screams overwhelming evidence of a loving, gracious God that didn't primarily send His Son to come and change what we do, but rather to change the way He relates to us: through GRACE.

The veil was torn for believers to be able to enter into the holy of holies with confidence, not based on our own worthiness, but based on the perfect obedience of the one man, Jesus Christ, on our behalf. But through the centuries the church has sewed this veil right back up, depicting God as a harsh and unapproachable God. Jesus received the full punishment for our sins and we received the full reward for His perfect obedience and He imputed to us His Godly righteousness:

> *For He made Him who knew no sin to be sin for us, that we might become the righteousness of God in Him. (2 Cor 5:21 NKJV)*

We are not propagating immorality, because if we truly believe in God and love Him there will be corresponding works (because faith without works is dead). But the purpose with this book is to boldly preach the message of God's unconditional love and acceptance in spite of our mistakes, a message that in the past has been preached in a confusing cocktail mixed up with Old Covenant Law, the very thing Jesus died to set us free from. Good works and obedience have been preached AT THE COST OF GRACE, causing God's children to be robbed of their confidence before God and always left feeling somewhat unworthy.

We have been called to take back that ground.

www.NewCovenantGrace.com

Foreword by Author

<u>Growing Up</u>

I was raised in a very conservative Christian home by parents who loved me dearly and wanted me to have the best possible education. Firm moral ethics were the order of the day. My sister and I were taught that all our actions had consequences, to take responsibility for our decisions and to always give our very best at what we did.

I went through the motions of attending church and Sunday school every week (there is nothing wrong with exposing children to some good, solid Bible instruction) and then, as the tradition / rule of the church stipulated, we had to pass a written test which included quoting the 10 Commandments word for word from Exodus 20 in order to qualify for being confirmed as a member of the church. I scored the highest in the class with 98% and thought myself to be a very "good" Christian. However the very next week I found myself having lustful thoughts and I spent the night on my knees, crying out to God for forgiveness because I was now a sinner again, fearing that I would be thrown into hell if I were to die that night.

Through this and many more similar experiences I learned to relate to God on the basis of my own level of obedience, which meant that if I had a good week, my relationship with God would be thriving; but if I had a bad week, I would feel too guilty to even talk with Him. Even if I could muster up the courage to get down on my knees, it would be with the attitude of a murderer pleading for mercy before a harsh judge.

I could never seem to get victory over bad habits, even though I'd been a born again believer for years. Sin and temptation seemed to plague me around every corner, but I kept that well hidden from the many people whom expected me to be living a holy "Christian" life.

Realizing My Folly

I was a hypocrite, on my way to becoming a modern day Pharisee. I distinctly remember the one instance while I was studying Mechanical Engineering at Johannesburg University and living in the men's residence. I walked into the communal hall where everybody cooked their food and hung out together. As I walked in, one of the guys whom I knew suddenly hid the cigarette he was smoking behind his back. Confused, I asked him why he did that. His reply was that he did not want me to see him smoking, thinking that I'd be disappointed with him because I was on the "Spiritual Care Committee" of the residence at that time.

It appeared that I had been passing judgment on people who seemed to be committing "bigger sins" than me, thinking that my superior level of morality made me a better person and therefore also made me more loved by God. Clearly I didn't understand the following verse yet:

> For whoever shall keep the whole law, and yet stumble in one
> point, he is guilty of all. (Jam 2:10 NKJV)

This should have been a clear indication that our own level of morality has nothing to do with it...

At the time I would study the scriptures every day because I loved God and had a passion for His kingdom. But even though I gained a lot of knowledge about God, I was never able to maintain "right standing" with Him for more than a few days at a time, because my relationship with Him was based on how well I performed. And since I made mistakes every day, my conscience always accused me and drove me away from Him whenever I messed up.

One day in 2002 a friend took four of us into his room, had us sit down and said he wanted to share something with us that might seem like blasphemy, but said that God had shown it to him the previous week. He only got as far as "We are not under the 10 Commandments anymore" when my mind began kicking and screaming to get out of the room!! He tried explaining to us how the finished work of the cross and the blood of Jesus had completely set us free from the Old Covenant Law, and he was right: I thought he was blaspheming!!!

I made a resolution not to have too much to do with him from that day on and considered him very unfortunate to have been brainwashed by some mysterious group of "fringe fanatic Christians". Looking back now, I can clearly see that he was posing a threat to my religious convictions and my lack of knowledge of Bible truth made me fearful of anything that tried to rock my little boat.

Glorious Grace!

Then I married a princess by the name of Natalie in 2006 and in the beginning of 2007 we relocated to Hong Kong for work. We went "church-hunting" and in the process through mutual friends were introduced to a church called *City Church International*¹ led by Rob and Glenda Rufus (who also happened to be South Africans). They had planted the church there just a few years earlier after serving on the leadership of *Coastlands Church* in Adelaide, Australia, for several years.

We continued to visit because the people all seemed so happy and made us feel very welcome. After a few weeks I became intrigued by the preaching coming from the pulpit, because this little pastor from Africa seemed to have answers for all those "problem" verses in the Bible that I had always wondered about.

Then after about three months we finally decided to commit to that church and its vision. Week after week I sat there hungrily drinking the pure water of life as though it was the first time I had ever sat in a church! The lights came on in many areas of my mind and I began to sense a massive change within me: The undiluted, uncompromised message of grace that was being preached began chipping away at my law-based mindset which comprised of a framework of self righteous rituals that I had set up to try and manipulate God to approve of me. I had run that treadmill of performance as best as I could for the first 26 years of my life and yet my best efforts never seemed to appease it.

And here, for the first time, the picture finally began to dawn on me: He loves me unconditionally apart from my performance; He loves me so much that He gave His only Son to be nailed to a cross for me and He did it before I had even loved Him and while I was still an "enemy" of God!

It took nearly all my self control not to walk out the door at times, as Rob's preaching can get pretty intense and "in your face" at times. But the volumes of truth coming from his mouth far outweighed the offense and rebellious cries coming from my unrenewed mind.

Growing in Grace

I got my hands on as many sermons from people who preached this grace message as I could. I listened to it when I traveled to work, to friends and to appointments. I listened to it on my iPod during my lunch breaks, at gym, whenever I traveled, before I went to bed, talked about it with friends, my pastor, my wife, prayed about it, dreamt about it and wrote songs about it. I couldn't get enough! The truth was intoxicating and I sensed that I had finally found what I had been searching for my whole life: a revelation of unfaltering right standing with God.

For about 26 years of my life I had managed to "miss" verses in the Bible such as:

I do not set aside the grace of God; for if righteousness comes through the law, then Christ died in vain. (Gal 2:21 NKJV)

Therefore we conclude that a man is justified by faith apart from the deeds of the law. (Rom 3:28 NKJV)

Having wiped out the handwriting of requirements that was against us, which was contrary to us. And He has taken it out of the way, having nailed it to the cross. (Col 2:14 NKJV)

For Christ is the end of the law for righteousness to everyone who believes. (Rom 10:14 NKJV)

Grace from Beginning to End

Why is it that we always tell unbelievers and sinners that the only thing they need to do to be saved, is to believe in Jesus Christ? That's it, simple as that! But then once they start coming to church, we suddenly change our story and tell them that they'd better stop doing this or that thing because God will punish them. How dare we move the goal posts like that?

We tell them that they can get saved through faith, but then they have to *stay saved* through their own fleshly efforts. This is exactly what Paul warned the churches in Galatia against:

O foolish Galatians! Who has bewitched you that you should not obey the truth, before whose eyes Jesus Christ was clearly portrayed among you as crucified? This only I want to learn from you: Did you receive the Spirit by the works of the law, or by the hearing of faith? Are you so foolish? Having begun in the Spirit, are you now being made perfect by the flesh? (Gal 3:1-3 NKJV)

Also to the Colossians:

As you therefore have received Christ Jesus the Lord, so walk in Him. (Col 2:6 NKJV)

Just as we have received Him (by faith in Christ alone), so we should continue to walk in Him: relating to God through faith in Christ alone and *not* through our own efforts of self righteousness. Have you actually seen how the Bible describes *our* efforts to try and be righteous before God through our own works?

But we are all like an unclean thing, and all our righteousnesses are like filthy rags. (Isa 64:6a NKJV)

It is only through the obedience of the one man, Jesus Christ and *His* righteousness given to us a free gift, that we can stand perfect before God.

Why This Book?

My purpose with writing this book is for it to be an account of topics and doctrines that I have personally struggled with, but which God has revealed to me through the ministry of the Holy Spirit and the obedience of men such as Rob Rufus, Joseph Prince, Steve McVey, Bill Johnson, Andrew Wommack, Andrew Farley, Cornel Marais, Paul Ellis, Bertie Brits, Tony Ide and Curry Blake, to name but a few.

I count myself as privileged to be able to stand on the shoulders of these giants and learn from them, and dedicate this book to all the people who have inspired me through their selfless devotion to spreading the fragrance of the grace of God through the nations.

My prayer is for this book to destroy the religious arguments and doctrines of demons forever, to irrefutably prove from scripture that the Old Covenant Law of Moses was nailed to the cross with Jesus over 2000 years ago and that we, as New Covenant believers, have been given "unfair" advantages in life over the people living in subjection to the beggarly elements of this world (Galatians 4).

Grace has empowered me to live free from condemnation and the fear of punishment, giving me the boldness to enter into the holy of holies and with an unveiled face behold the glory of my Father, who loves me with a love beyond what I'm able to put into words.

> *There is no fear in love; but perfect love casts out fear, because fear involves torment. But he who fears has not been made perfect in love. (1 John 4:18 NKJV)*

Grace also empowers us to do greater exploits for God than we were ever able to do under law. In December 2008 my wife and I relocated to Perth, Australia and joined a sister church of our Hong Kong Church, *Freedom Life*[2], led by loving shepherds Tony and Robyn Ide, whom we've grown to love very much. Over this period I made a commitment to write a weekly devotional message that I would send out to whoever wanted to read it. People were weekly subscribing by the dozens and this has led to the creation of the ministry called *New Covenant Grace*[3] that has touched the lives of many people across the world.

In March 2010 we moved back to our home country, South Africa, where we currently reside. The fragrance of grace is spreading like a wildfire among our friends and family and we are excited about what lies ahead!

How to Grow in Grace

If you ever wish to renew your mind at an accelerated rate and learn to have discipline to go and search the scriptures for truth to refute the arguments of the modern day Pharisees, I would encourage you to start writing a blog or begin your own website or a discussion group on a social networking site like Facebook, sharing truth with people as God reveals it to you. Throw yourself into the thick of things and watch God work through you! Sometimes we only realize *why* we take a stand for certain things when we have to defend it.

The quickest way to learn is on the job and not by sitting on the sidelines. Every time the legalists have come with their piercing questions, it has forced me to go and look for the answers and to question why I hold on so dearly to my beliefs. In the end it has only served to strengthen my resolve. But probably the most notable thing is the way how I've fallen in love with Jesus through all this. Reading the Bible isn't just reading anymore. There are few things that compare to the wonder of having the veil of the law removed and reading God's love letter through the perspective of what Jesus accomplished on the cross.

I can also not overstress the importance of downloading sermons from the dozens of free resources available on the internet and soak under the teachings of people who have gone further down the road than us. Most of us have spent years and years having our heads filled with all sorts of garbage from people who thought they were speaking the truth. Ridding ourselves of all these thought patterns, habits and ideas doesn't happen overnight. It takes patience and time to unlearn ideas and thoughts that have been drilled into our minds over the years.

I have included links to some of these websites at the end of this book.

Two Components of Grace

Lastly I would like to make a statement that I hope will clarify a lot of things for people. Grace has two components, namely *Acceptance Grace* and *Empowerment Grace*:

Acceptance Grace is the way we relate to God, namely through the perfect obedience of Jesus Christ on our behalf. This component of grace is the foundation of the gospel. Grace came in the form of a person, namely Jesus Christ.

> For *the law was given* through Moses, but *grace and truth came* through Jesus Christ. (John 1:17 NKJV, emphasis added)

The law was given from a distance (impersonally), but grace *came* personally and dwelled among us.

The apostle Paul took great care to build his gospel on the foundation of grace (who is Christ) in all the early churches:

> *According to the grace of God which was given to me, as a wise master builder I have laid the foundation, and another builds on it. But let each one take heed how he builds on it. For no other foundation can anyone lay than that which is laid, which is Jesus Christ. (1 Cor 3:10-11 NKJV)*

We ALWAYS need to relate to God in this way, because this is the only way that He relates to us.

Empowerment Grace is that supernatural enabling which allows us to do things that would normally be beyond our natural ability or effort. As we are swallowed up by God's amazing grace and we begin to get rid of the *"I have to"* mentality, we find a breathtaking *"I want to"* attitude that begins to rise up inside us, which is of course the Holy Spirit communicating His desire to live through us, endowing us with all of heaven's infinite resources and aspirations.

We are the vessels through which God wants to show Himself strong; we are the channels through which He wants His power to flow; we are His conductors through which heaven invades the earth, allowing the Father's will to be done in this broken world. This is the essence of *Empowerment Grace*.

Spiritual Immaturity

This book is essentially about *Acceptance Grace*, about being established in righteousness. Like Rob Rufus says: "You cannot see the promised land while living in the land of slavery". In order to explore the depths of God's love and His kindness towards us, to go further and also discover the wonders of the *New Creation* and *Empowerment Grace*, we firstly need to be firmly rooted in *Acceptance Grace*, which the apostle Paul calls "the word of righteousness":

> *For though by this time you ought to be teachers, you need someone to teach you again the first principles of the oracles of God; and you have come to need milk and not solid food. For everyone who partakes only of milk is unskilled in the <u>word of righteousness</u>, for he is a babe. (Heb 5:12-13 NKJV, emphasis added)*

I remained unskilled in the word of righteousness for years and years of my life even though I knew I had been saved by grace. The symptoms of being unskilled in the word of righteousness are easy to detect:

1. You constantly need someone to tell you that God still loves you and even though you know this, you don't really *believe* it.

2. You are never really sure that if you were to die right now that you are actually going to heaven.

3. You lack confidence in approaching God because of guilt about something you've done.

4. You mostly feel that you are not doing enough for God to be pleased with you; etc. The list goes on and on...

It is impossible for anybody to truly know God without understanding righteousness, grace and the New Covenant. I trust that this book will go a long way in removing the confusion that exists in the church about the true nature of God and that it will help you, the reader, to approach Him with boldness and confidence because you have been made righteous and holy for ever through the finished work of the cross, even though your behavior may not always look like it.

I have written this book as a series of short messages, outlining the basic principles of each topic. Read them SLOWLY, even if a Bible verse seems all too familiar to you. Occasionally I have also inserted my own words inside a Bible verse to emphasize a particular point that I would like to bring across, like this:

> *"For a mere moment I have forsaken you* [when we were still under the law], *But with great mercies I will gather you." (Isa 54:7 NKJV, annotations added)*

I have also included links to several articles on the Internet for those who would like to read more about a certain topic; I can not guarantee however the continued availability of these websites at any point in future. They can be found at the back of this book.

You may also find several verses and concepts being repeated over and over again. I would encourage you not to skip or merely glance over these, but rather use them to reinforce the message of grace into the fibers of your very inner being.

We are humbled by what God is doing through His Word, and we trust that you too would be encouraged to see the whole new realm of grace, freedom, power and joy in the Holy Spirit!

In Grace
Andre van der Merwe
www.NewCovenantGrace.com

To my wife, Natalie

Thank you for standing by my side every step of our journey.

I could not have hoped for a better life partner to accompany me on this adventure.

I love you always…

Law →✝→ Grace

Three Covenants

There are many covenants in the Bible, but here we will only focus on three, the first two being covenants which God had made with man and the third one which was made within the Trinity itself. If we comprehend these three covenants it will make the Bible much clearer and simpler to understand. Firstly however we must understand the difference between a covenant and a promise:

When God makes a promise, we have to put our faith in that promise for it to come to pass:

> ...but imitate those <u>who through faith</u> and patience <u>inherit the promises</u>. (Heb 6:12 NKJV, emphasis added)

> ...<u>who through faith</u> subdued kingdoms, worked righteousness, <u>obtained promises</u>, stopped the mouths of lions. (Heb 11:33 NKJV, emphasis added)

However, when God makes a covenant it *will* come to pass, whether we believe it or not. God can not lie and when He takes an oath, He always does what He says. Let's look at those three covenants:

First Covenant

God appears to Abraham and makes a covenant to be Abraham's God and to multiply and bless him.

> Then Abram fell on his face, and God talked with him, saying: "As for Me, behold, My covenant is with you, and you shall be a father of many nations. No longer shall your name be called Abram, but your name shall be Abraham; for I have made you a father of many nations. I will make you exceedingly fruitful; and I will make

1

> *nations of you, and kings shall come from you. And I will establish*
> *My covenant between Me and you and your descendants after you*
> *in their generations, for an everlasting covenant, to be God to you*
> *and your descendants after you. (Gen 17:3-7 NKJV)*

There were no strings attached. Abraham also didn't do anything to deserve any of this; he didn't keep any laws or live unusually holy. As a matter of fact, some theological scholars believe Abraham was an Iraqi who worshipped pagan Gods! He disobeyed God by sleeping with his wife's servant (Hagar) and through this single act of disobedience gave birth to Ishmael, who became the father of all the Arab nations as we know them today. His wife Sarah later gave birth to Isaac, the son who was born according to the promise and who became the father of the Israelites. And we know that up to this day there exists a continuous conflict between these nations.

Abraham also lied twice about his wife Sarah (once to the Pharaoh in Genesis 12 and once to Abimelech the king of Gerar, in Genesis 20) and alleged that she was his sister. Abraham was afraid that they would kill him due to the fact that she was a very beautiful woman.

Now even though Abraham was clearly in the wrong here, God didn't rebuke him for it but instead rebuked the pharaoh!

> *But the LORD plagued Pharaoh and his house with great plagues*
> *because of Sarai, Abram's wife. (Gen 12:17 NKJV)*

And later *again* God rebuked the king of Gerar and *not* Abraham:

> *But God came to Abimelech in a dream by night, and said to him,*
> *"Indeed you are a dead man because of the woman whom you have*
> *taken, for she is a man's wife". (Gen 20:3 NKJV)*

Who was in the wrong here? Abraham! Who did God rebuke? The king! This was because God had established a covenant with Abraham and neither with the pharaoh nor the king. And because God *always* keeps His part of the bargain, Abraham was favored by God because of this covenant.

We just saw that Abraham had lied about his wife, but because of God's blessing on his life he came out of Egypt (and later also out of Gerar) laden with slaves and cattle and wealth! Now by this we are not saying that people should go out and lie to other people and deceive them in order for God to bless them! We are by no means endorsing immoral living, but this just serves to illustrate that God blessed Abraham regardless of his level of obedience. God blessed Abraham even though he lied!

There was no moral standard to live up to, since the Law of Moses which included the 10 Commandments was only introduced 430 years later, which brings us to the second covenant.

Second Covenant

This is described in the Bible as the "Old Covenant", where God gave the law and the 10 Commandments to Moses.

Israel had kept on murmuring and complaining ever since God had led them out of Egypt with mighty signs and wonders. They also didn't want to have a personal relationship with God, but instead always asked Moses to speak to God on their behalf. They were uncomfortable with having to "deal" with God personally and preferred to remain at a distance. Despite of all the goodness that God had shown them they always kept on murmuring and complaining, even saying that God and Moses wanted to kill them!

> *And the children of Israel said to them, "Oh, that we had died by the hand of the LORD in the land of Egypt, when we sat by the pots of meat and when we ate bread to the full! For you have brought us out into this wilderness to kill this whole assembly with hunger. (Ex 16:3 NKJV)*

The tragedy of this is that in Exodus 15 (the previous chapter) Israel had just sung a song about the goodness of God and about how He had delivered them from the Egyptians when the waters of the Red Sea closed over them. And here in the very next chapter they accuse Him of wanting to kill them!

This happened again and again, time after time. Eventually, because Israel refused to believe that God was on their side, He gave them the law and all the other commandments to keep, something that didn't require any faith from their side (faith in God's goodness):

> *Then he* [Moses] *took the Book of the Covenant and read in the hearing of the people. And they* [Israel] *said, "All that the LORD has said we will do, and be obedient." And Moses took the blood, sprinkled it on the people, and said, "This is the blood of the covenant which the LORD has made with you according to all these words". (Ex 24:7-8 NKJV, annotations added)*

The Sin of Unbelief

In Galatians 3 we read more about *why* the law was given to Israel:

3

> *What purpose then does the law serve? It was added because of transgressions, till the Seed should come to whom the promise was made. (Gal 3:19 NKJV)*

Israel's transgression was their persistent unbelief in the goodness of God. They blindly refused to acknowledge that God wanted to bless them, love them, care for them and be their God. So the law was given unto them, but only for a *certain period.* God already had a master plan to restore mankind back into unbroken fellowship with Himself and He knew that the Old Law Covenant would only be in power *until the Seed* should come. This Seed, of course, was Jesus Christ.

> *For who, having heard, rebelled? Indeed, was it not all who came out of Egypt, led by Moses? Now with whom was He [God] angry forty years? Was it not with those who sinned, whose corpses fell in the wilderness? And to whom did He [God] swear that they would not enter His rest, but to those who did not obey? So we see that they could not enter in because of unbelief. (Heb 3:16-19 NKJV, annotations added)*

Note in the previous verses it talks about "those who sinned" and "they could not enter because of unbelief" (still talking about the same people, namely Israel).

Israel should never have agreed to living under the law! God would have accepted and loved them regardless of how holy (or unholy) they lived, because they were Abraham's descendants and we just read about God's amazing covenant with Abraham. God declared Abraham to be righteous simply because he believed God:

> *And he [Abraham] believed in the LORD, and He [the Lord] accounted it to him for righteousness. (Gen 15:6 NKJV, annotations added)*

But instead, Israel in their pride said:

> *"All that the LORD has spoken we will do, and we will be obedient." (Exo 24:7b ESV)*

> *Cursed is he who does not rise to all the Words of this Law, to do them! And all the people shall say, Amen! (Deut 27:26 LITV)*

They agreed to something they would never be able to do! This must rank right up there with the Garden of Eden in the list of all time dumb things said or done. Even God said about them:

> *And the LORD said to Moses, "I have seen this people, and indeed it is a stiff-necked people! (Ex 32:9 NKJV)*

God never originally meant for us to try to relate to Him in this way. Just after God's commands were written on stone and He set the choice of curse (for disobedience) or blessing (for obedience) before Israel, He said the following to Moses:

> *And the LORD said to Moses: "Behold, you will rest with your fathers; and this people will rise and play the harlot with the gods of the foreigners of the land, where they go to be among them, and they will forsake Me and break My covenant which I have made with them. (Deut 31:16 NKJV)*

Does this look like God's best plan for mankind? If even God Himself said that He *knew* Israel would break the Old Covenant Law, does it really seem logical that He would still want people to base their relationship with Him on the basis of how well they are able to obey a set of rules?

The Characteristics of a Covenant

One of the characteristics of a covenant is that it cannot be withdrawn from by either of the parties that made it, since a covenant is a life-long contract or agreement. For a covenant to end, either one of the parties that entered into it literally has to die. Since Israel was never able to fully keep up their side of the covenant and remain 100% obedient to *all* its stipulations, they were in breach of its requirements which meant that God had to keep up His side of the covenant and punish them for their disobedience.

All the horrible curses that would strike Israel for disobedience can be found in Deuteronomy 28:15-68. If God hadn't punished them for their sins, He would have been in breach of His side of the covenant, thereby making Him a liar and of course we know that God can not lie.

There was also another problem: Since God has an indestructible life, He could not bring an end to this covenant by dying Himself. He therefore had His Spirit conceive a child through a human woman and the man Jesus Christ was born into this world. Jesus Christ lived a 100% perfectly obedient life, thereby fulfilling *all* the requirements of the Old Covenant Law, which brings us to the third Covenant:

Third Covenant

This is the most amazing New Covenant under which we now live! This covenant was cut within the Trinity with no human influence or intervention, but purely out of God's heart of love towards us.

God took away the laws He gave to Moses, canceling the written code that stood opposed to us:

> *...having wiped out the handwriting of requirements that was against us, which was contrary to us. And He has taken it out of the way, having nailed it to the cross. (Col 2:14 NKJV)*

He made Jew, Greek and Gentile equal - God's church has now become spiritual Israel.

> *For he is not a Jew who is one outwardly, nor is circumcision that which is outward in the flesh; but he is a Jew who is one inwardly... (Rom 2:28-29a NKJV)*

God's relationship with Israel *before* the introduction of the Old Covenant was a type and shadow of what He wants to have with the whole world today.

> *...that is, that God was in Christ reconciling the world to Himself, not imputing their trespasses to them, and has committed to us the word of reconciliation. (2 Cor 5:19 NKJV, emphasis added)*

It is required that when making a covenant it has to be sealed with blood. God had also confirmed His covenant with Abraham with blood (Gen 15:9-18) and had Israel do the same:

> *Therefore not even the first covenant was dedicated without blood. For when Moses had spoken every precept to all the people according to the law, he took the blood of calves and goats, with water, scarlet wool, and hyssop, and sprinkled both the book itself and all the people, saying, "This is the blood of the covenant which God has commanded you." Then likewise he sprinkled with blood both the tabernacle and all the vessels of the ministry. And according to the law almost all things are purified with blood, and without shedding of blood there is no remission. (Heb 9:18-22 NKJV, emphasis added)*

In the Old Covenant Israel slaughtered animals to appease the wrath of God. In essence they were only postponing the punishment for their sins for another year, because the blood of animals could never fully serve as payment for the sins of mankind:

> *For it is not possible that the blood of bulls and goats could take away sins. (Heb 10:4 NKJV)*

So God sent His only Son, allowed Him to be crucified by the very people He came to save and accepted His blood as the full, perfect and complete payment for *all* the past, present and future sins of all mankind. The Father then entered into a New Covenant with His Son Jesus, stipulating that the righteousness and all the blessings that Jesus had earned through His perfect obedience were to be given as a free gift to mankind on one condition: They had to believe in Jesus Christ as their Lord and Savior. Every person that accepted Jesus' sacrifice as a full and complete payment for their sins would be imputed with the perfect righteousness of God Himself:

> *I will greatly rejoice in the LORD, My soul shall be joyful in my God; For He has clothed me with the garments of salvation, He has covered me with the robe of righteousness. (Isa 61:10a NKJV)*

God would also wipe out their sinfulness through the perfect offering of the cross, imparting His perfection unto all who believe in Him:

> *For by one offering He hath perfected for ever them that are sanctified. (Heb 10:14 KJV)*

Many people call this the "divine exchange" - our sinfulness was laid on Jesus and His righteousness was given to us as a free gift. Actually He was MADE to BE sin. Righteousness therefore wasn't just given to us: we BECAME righteousness!

> *For He made Him who knew no sin to be sin for us, that we might become the righteousness of God in Him. (2 Cor 5:21 NKJV)*

In fact the Bible is so full of references to the reality that the Old Covenant has passed away and that it has been replaced by the New Covenant, that it is very hard to miss it! The following verses clearly tell us that the Old Covenant (referring to the Law of Moses), which was only a type and a shadow of the New Covenant, has passed away:

> *For if that first covenant had been faultless, then no place would have been sought for a second. Because finding fault with them, He says: "Behold, the days are coming, says the LORD, when I will make a new covenant with the house of Israel and with the house of Judah* [remember how we spoke a little earlier about all believers being "Jews"?] - *not according to the covenant that I made with their fathers in the day when I took them by the hand to lead them out of the land of Egypt; because they did not continue in My covenant, and I disregarded them, says the LORD.*
>
> *For this is the covenant that I will make with the house of Israel after those days, says the LORD: I will put My laws in their mind and write them on their hearts* [this means God will give us the desire to please Him and have fellowship with Him, to seek His

heart for us]*; and I will be their God, and they shall be My people. None of them shall teach his neighbor, and none his brother, saying, 'Know the LORD,' for all shall know Me, from the least of them to the greatest of them.* [This means gone are the days where we need a priest or someone else to constantly tell us about God, now we can know Him personally and intimately!]

For I will be merciful to their unrighteousness, and their sins and their lawless deeds I will remember no more." [Do you really need any more proof that God won't ever punish you again?] *In that He says, "A new covenant," He has made the first obsolete. (Heb 8:7-13 NKJV, annotations and emphasis added)*

Beneficiaries of Two Covenants!

Now, when a person becomes born again through simply putting their faith in Jesus, they are grafted into "spiritual Israel" and God plants His own Seed inside them:

For you are all sons of God through faith in Christ Jesus. For as many of you as were baptized into Christ have put on Christ. There is neither Jew nor Greek, there is neither slave nor free, there is neither male nor female; for you are all one in Christ Jesus. And if you are Christ's, then you are Abraham's seed, and heirs according to the promise. (Gal 3:26-29 NKJV)

Here is verse 29 again, read it slowly:

And if you are Christ's, then you are Abraham's seed, and heirs according to the promise.

We not only become partakers of the New Covenant, inheriting all its wonderful benefits, but through our faith in Jesus we also become heirs of the promises that God made to Abraham! Talk about a double portion, shabba! Here are some more verses:

...just as Abraham "believed God, and it was accounted to him for righteousness." Therefore know that only those who are of faith are sons of Abraham. And the Scripture, foreseeing that God would justify the Gentiles by faith, preached the gospel to Abraham beforehand, saying, "In you all the nations shall be blessed." So then those who are of faith are blessed with believing Abraham. (Gal 3:6-9 NKJV)

> *You are sons of the prophets, and of the covenant which God made with our fathers, saying to Abraham, 'And in your seed all the families of the earth shall be blessed. (Acts 3:25 NKJV)*

> *Christ has redeemed us from the curse of the law, having become a curse for us (for it is written, "Cursed is everyone who hangs on a tree"), that the blessing of Abraham might come upon the Gentiles in Christ Jesus, that we might receive the promise of the Spirit through faith. (Gal 3:13-14 NKJV)*

God will never again refrain from doing good to us and even when He chastens us (Hebrews 12) it is an affectionate reproach from His heart of love.

Old Testament Prophesies

Some of the Old Testament prophets were given visions of the New Covenant and they painted an amazingly clear picture of the unconditional love of God towards His children; of a God that has chosen to blot out their sins and relate to them on the basis of the perfect obedience of His Son, Jesus Christ:

> *And I will make an everlasting covenant with them, that I will not turn away from doing them good; but I will put My fear in their hearts so that they will not depart from Me. (Jer 32:40 NKJV)*

> *And I will establish My covenant with you. Then you shall know that I am the LORD …when I provide you an atonement for all you have done," says the Lord GOD'". (Eze 16:62-63b NKJV)*

The blood of Jesus was the atonement:

> *For this is My blood of the new covenant, which is shed for many for the remission of sins. (Matt 26:28 NKJV)*

Probably the most well known prophesy that an Old Testament prophet made about the coming New Covenant is found in Isaiah 54:

> *"For a mere moment I have forsaken you* [when people were still under the law], *But with great mercies I will gather you. With a little wrath I hid My face from you for a moment* [God had to serve punishment for man's disobedience to the Old Law Covenant]; *But with everlasting kindness I will have mercy on you," Says the LORD, your Redeemer.* [What part of "everlasting kindness" is so hard to understand?] *"For this is like the waters of Noah to Me; For as I have sworn that the waters of Noah would no longer cover the earth, so have I sworn that I would not*

> *be angry with you, nor rebuke you* [There goes a whole heap of "angry God" theories and doctrines right out the door]. *For the mountains shall depart and the hills be removed, but My kindness shall not depart from you, nor shall My covenant of peace be removed," says the LORD, who has mercy on you. (Isaiah 54:7-10 NKJV, annotations added)*

Under which covenant will we choose to live?

Law →✝→ Grace

Matt 5:17-18 - Did Jesus End the Law or Not?

Many people who still believe they have to live according to the Old Covenant Laws have thrown Matthew 5:17-18 at preachers of the grace message to try and prove their case. But what does the Bible really say about living under the law and whether we are still bound to it?

> *"Do not think that I came to destroy the law or the Prophets. I did not come to destroy but to fulfill. For assuredly, I say to you, till Heaven and earth pass away, one jot or one tittle will by no means pass from the law till all is fulfilled. (Matt 5:17-18 NKJV)*

Peter Ditzel from Word of His Grace[1] explains these two verses as follows:

"Jesus is giving us two either / or conditions here: The law cannot pass until heaven and earth pass OR the law cannot pass until all is fulfilled. One or the other can do it. Heaven and earth have not yet passed, so we will leave that aside. But what did Jesus mean by ALL being fulfilled? He was referring to what He had just said in the previous sentence: the fulfilling or completing of the law AND the prophets. Once He had fulfilled the law and the prophets, the law could pass. Why is it that so many people who accept that Jesus fulfilled the Old Testament prophecies have a hard time understanding that in exactly the same way, He fulfilled the Old Testament laws: ALL of them?"

Legal Requirements of the Law

When a person is under a contractual obligation to someone else and they fulfill all the requirements of that contract, it means the contract is finished and over. But if they simply destroyed the contractual agreement before fulfilling its requirements, they are not released from its obligations, which is why Jesus said that He did not come to destroy the law. But the moment the obligations of the contract are fulfilled, that person is set free from it! In exactly the same way Jesus did not come to destroy the law, but He fulfilled it.

> *For Christ is the end of the law for righteousness to everyone who believes. (Rom 10:4 NKJV)*

Because all the righteous requirements of the law were fulfilled in Christ and since we are given the righteousness of Christ and filled with the Holy Spirit as a free gift when we put our faith in Jesus, it means that in Christ we too have fulfilled the requirements of the law and therefore the law has ended for us as well.

> *For what the law could not do, in that it was weak through the flesh, God sending his own Son in the likeness of sinful flesh, and for sin, condemned sin in the flesh: <u>That the righteousness of the law might be fulfilled in us</u>, who walk not after the flesh, but after the Spirit. (Rom 8:3-4 NKJV, emphasis added)*

If someone's mind has not been renewed to think in terms of grace, they might stare themselves blind against the last part of verse 4, thinking that we *have to* walk after the Spirit if we want to fulfill the righteous requirements of the law. But look down in verse 9:

> *But you are not in the flesh but in the Spirit, if indeed the Spirit of God dwells in you. Now if anyone does not have the Spirit of Christ, he is not His. (Rom 8:9 NKJV)*

This says that that if the Holy Spirit dwells in us, we are not in the flesh! So what these verses are actually saying is that if someone has the Holy Spirit inside them, it is proof that the requirements of the law *have been* met in them.

The Prophets

> *For all the prophets and the law prophesied until John. (Matt 11:13 NKJV)*

The entire law and the Old Testament Prophets spoke of the coming of the Messiah who would forgive the sins of the whole world. The law was our tutor (schoolmaster), teaching us "right living" until we should put our faith in Jesus and begin to live by faith.

> *But before faith came, we were kept under guard by the law, kept for the faith which would afterward be revealed. Therefore the law was our tutor to bring us to Christ, that we might be justified by faith. But after faith has come, we are no longer under a tutor. (Gal 3:23-25 NKJV)*

This says that after we've put our faith in Jesus Christ, we don't need the tutor of the law to instruct us anymore. The Holy Spirit inside us can do the job pretty well on His own - He doesn't need the assistance of an external set of rules!

> "*The law and the prophets were until John. <u>Since that time</u> the kingdom of God has been preached, and everyone is pressing into it*". (Luk 16:16 NKJV, emphasis added)

This verse implies that if we still preach law-based living we are *not* preaching the Kingdom, because we would be preaching things that ended with John the Baptist over 2000 years ago - read the verse again. How much clearer can it get?

> *Now to Abraham <u>and his Seed</u> were the promises made. He does not say, "And to seeds," as of many, but as of one, "And to your Seed," who is Christ.* (Gal 3:16 NKJV, emphasis added)

And also:

> *What then is the purpose of the law? It was added because of transgressions, <u>until the seed should come</u> to whom the promise was made; and it was ordained by angels in the hand of a mediator.* (Gal 3:19 NKJV, emphasis added)

These verses say that the law was given because of transgressions *until the Seed* should come (and Hebrews 3 tells us it was specifically the sin of unbelief). Then when the *Seed* (Christ) came, the law was fulfilled and we were freed from its legal requirements.

> *But now the righteousness of God <u>apart from the law</u> is revealed, being witnessed by the Law and the Prophets.* (Rom 3:21 NKJV, emphasis added)

If there were such a thing as the "court of heaven", the law and prophets would have stood up as witnesses, pointed their fingers to those who put their faith in Jesus and said: "That person is righteous!" Also note the verse says that this righteousness comes *apart* from the law.

From these verses and many more it is plain to see that believers are not supposed to try and live under the law anymore, but instead live by faith in Jesus Christ.

<u>Living in Sin</u>

Here is a shocker, something that should silence the mouths of those who still try to be justified by obeying the law. Let's look at two verses first:

> *And the law is not of faith… (Gal 3:12a NKJV)*

and

> *…for whatsoever is not of faith is sin. (Rom 14:23b NKJV)*

It's quite surprising to see what it says when we combine these two verses. Since the law is not of faith Galatians 3:12) and since anything that is not of faith is sin (Romans 14:23), it means that those who try to be justified by their own good works and try to live up to the moral code of the law are actually living in sin!

<u>Righteousness which Exceeds that of the Pharisees</u>

Jesus also said the following:

> *For I say to you, that unless your righteousness exceeds the righteousness of the scribes and Pharisees, you will by no means enter the kingdom of Heaven. (Matt 5:20 NKJV)*

The scribes and Pharisees prided themselves in how well they kept the laws of Moses; in fact it's what they did for a living! These laws didn't just include the 10 Commandments, but also all the rituals and daily sacrifices and a total of 613 stipulations and commandments that were contained in the five books of Moses (Genesis to Deuteronomy)[2].

In fact most people who try to live up to the Law of Moses today would pale in comparison against an average Pharisee. It is therefore simple to see that the righteousness which Jesus was talking about was not about believers trying to live more obedient or more holy; He was talking about a righteousness that comes from God, given to every believer as a free gift at the point of salvation. At the exact same moment that a believer puts their faith in Jesus, they are given His perfect righteousness and He is given their sin and transgressions:

> *For He made Him who knew no sin to be sin for us, that we might become the righteousness of God in Him. (2 Cor 5:21 NKJV)*

Isn't that just an amazing deal? Thank You Jesus!

Law →✝→ Grace

The Law Arouses Sin

If a married man were to go on a business trip to a different country and one night after work, while he was sitting in a pub sipping a drink, he was approached by a very attractive woman with "cruel intentions", what would be this man's motive for staying true to his wife? The ring on his finger? The piece of paper that he signed on his wedding day? No! These external things will never keep a person from committing adultery. The strongest motivation for the husband to remain true to his wife would be if he loved her.

It is exactly the same with Christians and holy living. The fact that a Christian *ought* to love their neighbor simply because the Bible says so is not enough motivation for them to actually do it. In fact most people perform rather poorly at things they *ought* to do, and much better at things they *want* to do.

It is a fact that when we tell somebody they are not allowed to do something, we are actually arousing a desire inside them that wants to do that very thing! This is exactly what the law does. People would not have known what sin was if it were not for the law, because the law says "don't do this" or "don't touch that":

> *What shall we say then? Is the law sin? Certainly not! On the contrary, I would not have known sin except through the law. For I would not have known covetousness unless the law had said, "You shall not covet." But sin, taking opportunity by the commandment, produced in me all manner of evil desire. (Rom 7:7-8 NKJV)*

Salvation = Moral Living?

One of the predominant doctrines doing the rounds in the church today regarding moral living, is that if a person is not performing very well morally we should probably question if they were really saved in the first place, or whether God can use them at all.

15

However it's really not our prerogative to stand in front of one of God's children (who may just be going through a rough time), point our finger and say "I don't think they are really saved". Who are we to judge? Chances are good that such a brother or sister might be sitting under the teaching of a person or ministry that is still preaching holy living and moral behavior modification at the cost of being unconditionally accepted and loved by God and this might be causing them to struggle with some bad habit or pattern of immorality. The Bible actually tells us to restore such a person with gentleness:

> *Brethren, if a man is overtaken in any trespass, you who are spiritual restore such a one in a spirit of gentleness, considering yourself lest you also be tempted. (Gal 6:1 NKJV)*

However when someone who claims to be saved, carries on in the same destructive lifestyle patterns for years and years and simply pops into church when it's convenient for a religious little Sunday morning "fix", with their lives void of any passion for God, it might be a good idea to talk to them about whether they were really saved in the first place.

But back to the point, a definite indication of legalism is when upholding some moral standard or code is considered to be more important than the person struggling with upholding it. In some circles where people call themselves Christians, people are actually thrown out from their midst if they commit a certain type of mistake.

> *Now the works of the flesh are evident, which are: adultery, fornication, uncleanness, lewdness, idolatry, sorcery, hatred, contentions, jealousies, outbursts of wrath, selfish ambitions, dissensions, heresies, envy, murders, drunkenness, revelries... (Gal 5:19-21a NKJV)*

From this verse it is interesting to see that the Bible lists drinking too much beer or wine up there with murder. Although we shouldn't condone this kind of behavior, we are not to pass judgment on anybody either, because we do not always understand their circumstances.

Contrary to popular belief however, telling people that they *don't* have to obey the laws of Moses anymore actually helps them to have more victory over sin, because it lifts the mould of external behavior modification off them. At salvation God gives us a 100% righteous born again spirit man on the inside that *wants* to live for God, *wants* to love other people and *wants* to do good.

Ryan Rufus from New Nature Publications[1] (Hong Kong) says: *"Any true believer will admit that if they had the choice to push a button that would allow them to never sin again, they would push that button in an instant."*

This is proof that the laws of God have now been written on our hearts and that we don't need the external written code (the law) to direct us anymore:

> *...I will put My laws in their mind and write them on their hearts* [this means God gave us the desire to please Him and have fellowship with Him]*; and I will be their God, and they shall be My people. (Heb 8:10b NKJV, annotations added)*

The laws referred to in this verse are not the 10 Commandments either, since we are living under a new and better covenant and not under the Old Covenant anymore.

Before we came to faith in Christ, the law was our schoolmaster that taught us "holy living" and was only a type and a shadow of the real thing, namely faith in Christ. The law, like a signpost, was only supposed to point us to the real thing - we were never supposed to set up camp next to the signpost!

> *Therefore the law was our tutor to bring us to Christ, that we might be justified by faith. But after faith has come, we are no longer under a tutor. (Gal 3:24-25 NKJV)*

The Bible calls the law (that was written on tablets of stone) the "ministry of death":

> *But if the <u>ministry of death</u>, written and engraved on stones, was glorious, so that the children of Israel could not look steadily at the face of Moses because of the glory of his countenance, which glory was passing away, how will the ministry of the Spirit not be more glorious? (2 Cor 3:7-8 NKJV, emphasis added).*

If we now tell people that they should live up to the demands of this Old Covenant System, it means that we are actually putting death on them.

To conclude, if people think that we are saying they can just go out and live in full blown depravity, licentiousness and immorality, simply running like animals after the desires of their flesh, *then they are wrong*. If God has removed our old sinful nature with its lustful desires, why would we want to live in it any longer?

> *...knowing this, that our old man was crucified with Him, that the body of sin might be done away with, that we should no longer be slaves of sin. (Rom 6:6 NKJV)*

Just as we once followed like slaves after the lusts of our old sinful nature, we now have the desire and privilege to follow the desires of our new 100% righteous reborn spirit:

I speak in human terms because of the weakness of your flesh. For just as you presented your members as slaves of uncleanness, and of lawlessness leading to more lawlessness, so now present your members as slaves of righteousness for holiness. (Rom 6:19 NKJV)

Law →✝→ Grace

When Did the Old Testament End?

The Bible speaks numerous times about believers being *heirs* of God, or about them having an *inheritance*.

> *And if we are children, then we are heirs; heirs of God and joint-heirs with Christ; so that if we suffer with Him, we may also be glorified together. (Rom 8:17 NKJV)*

> *...giving thanks to the Father, who has made us meet to be partakers of the inheritance of the saints in light. (Col 1:12 NKJV)*

Now it logically follows that in order for us to become heirs of God, He had to have a testament that specified that we would inherit from Him. The Bible has two Testaments, namely the Old and New Testament. Both the Hebrew and Greek words used for "testament" in the Bible can also be translated to mean "covenant". Whenever the context had to do with relationship, it was translated as "covenant". Whenever the context was about inheritance, it was translated as "testament":

G1242 διαθήκη *dee-ath-ay'-kay*

From G1303; properly a *disposition*, that is, (specifically) a *contract* (especially a devisory *will*): - covenant, testament.

It is common logic that if a person goes to their attorney and requests to draw up a new testament or to make changes to their current one, that the old one is rendered invalid. In the same way God drew up His Old Testament, but later established a new one to replace it! We'll get to the scriptures to prove this shortly.

In Genesis 12, 15, 17 and 22 we see God instating a covenant / testament with Abraham. It is important to see that initially the *only* heirs of this testament were

Abraham and his natural descendants, who were called the Hebrews, who later also become known as Israel and still later were called Jews. The inheritance that God gave to them was the Promised Land, a geographical area called Canaan.

In short this was the entire Old Testament. Neither the Philistines, the Assyrians, the Egyptians nor any other nation became heirs under the Old Testament, because we see God in numerous instances acting *against* these nations *in favor* of Israel – the only nation who inherited under the Old Testament.

Moses later also became the mediator of the Old Covenant made between God and the nation of Israel. God gave them the law which enforced the Old Covenant and it was upheld by the blood of animal sacrifices:

> *Therefore not even the first covenant was dedicated without blood. For when Moses had spoken every precept to all the people according to the law, he took the blood of calves and of goats, with water and scarlet wool and hyssop, and sprinkled both the book itself, and all the people, saying, "This is the blood of the covenant which God has commanded you". (Heb 9:18-20 NKJV)*

Jesus' Superior Blood

In Hebrews 9 we see a stark contrast being drawn between the blood of animals (which in essence kept the Old Covenant alive) and the blood of Jesus, the spiritual "animal" (have you ever wondered why Jesus was called the Lamb of God?) offered as a perfect *once for all* sacrifice for sin:

> *For if the blood of bulls and goats and the ashes of a heifer, sprinkling the unclean, sanctifies for the purifying of the flesh, how much more shall the blood of Christ, who through the eternal Spirit offered Himself without spot to God, cleanse your conscience from dead works to serve the living God? (Heb 9:13-14 NKJV)*

And also in Hebrews 10:

> *For it is not possible that the blood of bulls and goats could take away sins. (Heb 10:4 NKJV)*

> *And every priest stands ministering daily and offering repeatedly the same sacrifices, which can never take away sins. But this Man, after He had offered one sacrifice for sins for ever, sat down at the right hand of God, from that time waiting till His enemies are made His footstool. For by one offering He has perfected for ever those who are being sanctified. (Heb 10:11-14 NKJV)*

All Nations Included In The New Covenant

Later in Galatians 3 we see that God made a New Testament that drew all the nations of the earth into the covenant which God had made with Abraham:

> *Now to Abraham and his Seed were the promises made. He does not say, "And to seeds," as of many, but as of one, "And to your Seed," who is Christ. (Gal 3:16 NKJV)*

> *There is neither Jew nor Greek, there is neither slave nor free, there is neither male nor female; for you are all one in Christ Jesus. And if you are Christ's, then you are Abraham's seed, and heirs according to the promise. (Gal 3:28-29 NKJV)*

Nowhere under the Old Testament was any command given to Israel to spread and preach the gospel to any other nation on the earth, because only Israel were heirs under the Old Testament. But under the New Testament in Matthew 28:19 (after the cross) we have the great commission where the disciples were commanded to take the gospel to *all* the nations. Jesus became the mediator of a New Covenant or Testament, writing it in His own blood (not the blood of animals):

> *And for this reason He is the Mediator of the <u>new covenant</u>, by means of death, for the redemption of the transgressions under the first covenant, that those who are called may receive the promise of the eternal inheritance. (Heb 9:15, emphasis added)*

When Does a Testament Come Into Effect?

A testament or will only comes into power whenever somebody dies. In essence an heir cannot inherit if the testator (person who wrote the testament) is still alive.

> *In the case of a will it is necessary to prove that the person who made it has died, for a will means nothing while the person who made it is alive; it goes into effect only after his death. (Heb 9:16-17 GNB)*

Now consider this: During the 30 years or so that Jesus lived on the earth and the three years that He ministered before He died, under which testament did He live? Under the old of course! He was still alive and we just saw in the previous two verses that a testament does not come into effect while the person who wrote it is still alive.

21

Some people claim that they still have to obey the Old Covenant Law simply because Jesus did it. Well Jesus *had to* obey it because He was born under the Old Testament and had to fulfill it!

> But when the right time finally came, God sent his own Son. He came as the son of a human mother and lived under the Jewish Law. (Gal 4:4 GNB)

During His time on the earth we never see Jesus preaching the gospel of the Kingdom to anybody other than the Jews, because He was still living under the Old Testament and He wasn't allowed to share any of Israel's inheritance with non Jewish people. One time though we see Jesus venturing to a geographical area outside of Galilee and running into a Canaanite woman, who wasn't a Jew:

> Then Jesus went out from there and departed to the region of Tyre and Sidon. And behold, a woman of Canaan came from that region and cried out to Him, saying, "Have mercy on me, O Lord, Son of David! My daughter is severely demon-possessed." But He answered her not a word. And His disciples came and urged Him, saying, "Send her away, for she cries out after us." But He answered and said, "I was not sent except to the lost sheep of the house of Israel." Then she came and worshiped Him, saying, "Lord, help me!" But He answered and said, "It is not good to take the children's bread and throw it to the little dogs." And she said, "Yes, Lord, yet even the little dogs eat the crumbs which fall from their masters' table." Then Jesus answered and said to her, "O woman, great is your faith! Let it be to you as you desire." And her daughter was healed from that very hour. (Matt 15:21-28 NKJV)

In essence the woman was saying: "Lord if there is any surplus left of God's blessings, please help me!" And by faith this woman was grafted into the New Covenant even before it was time for the Gentiles to become partakers! We also see a few other similar examples in the Bible like Rahab the prostitute who hid the spies in Jericho, Ruth the Moabite, Naaman the Syrian who was cleansed of leprosy after washing himself seven times in the Jordan at the instruction of Elijah, etc. By faith these people transcended time and received their inheritance long before it was actually due to become theirs.

So When Did The Old Testament *Really* End?

The crucifixion and death of Jesus Christ is described in Matthew 27, Mark 15, Luke 23 and John 19. If we take for example the book of Matthew and note that chapter 27 is where the New Testament came into effect (because this is where Jesus died), this implies that everything before Matt 27 was Old Testament because the New Testament hadn't been established yet! Therefore according to its legal validity the New Testament actually only begins in Matthew 27 (and Mark 15, Luke 23 and John 19, after the crucifixion). Everything before these chapters is *Old Testament.*

So if the New Testament began at Golgotha with the death of Jesus Christ (remember Hebrews 9:16-17 above), it must mean that the Old Testament had to have been cancelled somewhere before that. God would not just leave a covenant hanging up in the air. And if He did end the Old Covenant, then there is no more reason to *want* to live under the Old Testament Law. We find a prophecy pertaining to this made by the prophet Zachariah at about 520BC. We'll share the story interwoven with the scriptures:

God was the shepherd of the flock of Israel under the Old Covenant, caring for them with His staff that He called "Favor" (and another one called "Union").

> *Those who bought and sold the sheep hired me, and I became the shepherd of the sheep that were going to be butchered. I took two sticks: one I called "Favor" and the other "Unity." And I took care of the flock. (Zech 11:7 GNB)*

The staff called "Favor" symbolized the covenant He had made with the nation of Israel. The problem with this flock of sheep was that they were continually running after idols and persisted in rebelling against their Shepherd. Now the Shepherd had just about had enough and told them that He was going to quit.

> *Then I said to the flock, "I will not be your shepherd any longer. Let those die who are to die. Let those be destroyed who are to be destroyed. Those who are left will destroy one another" (Zech 11:9 GNB)*

He also requested that they pay Him for the services He had rendered, but if they didn't want to pay Him that they could just leave it.

> *I said to them, "If you are willing, give me my wages. But if not, keep them." So they paid me thirty pieces of silver as my wages. (Zech 11:12 GNB)*

And on the day that Jesus was betrayed for thirty pieces of silver by Judas Iscariot, God broke His staff and ended the covenant He had made with Israel.

> *Then I took the stick called "Favor" and broke it, to cancel the covenant which the LORD had made with all the nations. (Zech 11:10 GNB)*

If we look at the context of Zechariah 11 we will see "all the nations" only refer to Israel and Judah.

> *Then I broke the second stick, the one called "Unity," and the unity of Judah and Israel was shattered. (Zech 11:14 GNB)*

Now here's a real gem: Over five hundred years before Christ was betrayed, the prophet Zechariah spoke these words:

> *And the LORD said to me, "Throw it to the potter" - that princely price they set on me. So I took the thirty pieces of silver and threw them into the house of the LORD for the potter. (Zech 11:13 NKJV)*

Thirty pieces of silver was the commonly agreed price paid to an owner if his slave was injured while working for someone else and also the price that Jesus was betrayed for by Judas Iscariot. So we see God sarcastically say that they paid a "princely price" for Him. The Son of God was betrayed for the price of an injured slave! And then we see the following scripture in Matthew 27 (note the part about the "potter"):

> *Then Judas, His betrayer, seeing that He had been condemned, was remorseful and brought back the thirty pieces of silver to the chief priests and elders, saying, "I have sinned by betraying innocent blood." And they said, "What is that to us? You see to it!" Then he threw down the pieces of silver in the temple and departed, and went and hanged himself. But the chief priests took the silver pieces and said, "It is not lawful to put them into the treasury, because they are the price of blood." And they consulted together and bought with them the potter's field, to bury strangers in. (Matt 27:3-7 NKJV)*

See Zech 11:13 above again - the prophecy even described the potter's field!

We see therefore that the Old Testament came to an end when Jesus was betrayed for thirty pieces of silver and in the spiritual realm broke His staff that symbolized His covenant with Israel. But praise be to God that only several hours later He wrote a New Covenant with His own blood, a Testament that included all the nations of the earth and allowed us to become His children and heirs through faith in the sacrifice of Jesus Christ!

Law →✝→ Grace

The True Test of Your Gospel

Each person's belief in the gospel is influenced and shaped by their exposure to it and by the extent to which their mind has been renewed, but unfortunately also by the earthly traditions they still hold on to.

> ...making the Word of God of no effect through your tradition which you have delivered. (Mar 7:13 NKJV)

Paul the apostle, who wrote most of the New Testament, preached a gospel that was revealed to him directly from God.

> And, brothers, I make known to you the gospel which was preached by me, that it is not according to man. For I did not receive it from man, nor was I taught it except by a revelation of Jesus Christ. (Gal 1:11-12)

This gospel is known as the Gospel of Grace:

> But none of these things move me; nor do I count my life dear to myself, so that I may finish my race with joy, and the ministry which I received from the Lord Jesus, to testify to the gospel of the grace of God. (Acts 20:24 NKJV, emphasis added)

> I marvel that you are turning away so soon from Him who called you in the grace of Christ, to a different gospel. (Gal 1:6 NKJV, emphasis added)

> ...just as it is right for me to think this of you all, because I have you in my heart, inasmuch as both in my chains and in the defense and confirmation of the gospel, you all are partakers with me of grace. (Phil 1:7 NKJV, emphasis added)

> *Therefore they stayed there a long time, speaking boldly in the Lord, who was bearing witness to <u>the word of His grace</u>, granting signs and wonders to be done by their hands. (Acts 14:3 NKJV, emphasis added)*

> *So now, brethren, I commend you to God and to the <u>word of His grace</u>, which is able to build you up and give you an inheritance among all those who are sanctified. (Acts 20:32 NKJV, emphasis added)*

There is a flood of grace hitting our planet at the moment, with millions and millions of people waking up to the truth that we are not justified by observing the law or living up to some moral standard anymore, but simply by believing in Jesus Christ.

> *Therefore we conclude that a man is justified by faith without the works of the law. (Rom 3:28 NKJV)*

Just like Paul the apostle prophesied in Galatians 4 however, those who believe in this gospel of grace will be persecuted by those who want to be justified by their own works:

> *But then even as he born according to flesh* [Ishmael was the son born out of the flesh, which represents the works of the law] *<u>persecuted him born according to the Spirit</u>* [Isaac was the son born out of the promise, which represents grace], *so it is also now, (Gal 4:29 NKJV, annotations and emphasis added)*

And here is the true test of the gospel of grace: If the gospel we are preaching does not put us in danger of being misunderstood by the legalists, in the sense that they might think we are saying that people can just go out and sin as much as they want, then we are not preaching grace to the extent that Paul was preaching it.

True grace lifts the law off believers so completely that according to the legalists it sets us free in more ways than it *should*. Legalists believe that the moment you lift the law off a believer, he or she will simply run out and begin to live in full blown depravity and fall into all kinds of wickedness. But they forget that we have a born again spirit on the inside of us that *does not want to* live like that!

Paul had to defend the gospel of grace in the same way. We can see from the "question and answer" manner that much of the book of Romans was written in, that he was countering many of the arguments which the religious crowd of the day was throwing at him. They were probably accusing him of preaching that the believers, because they weren't under the law anymore, could go out and sin as much as they wanted! Here was Paul's reply:

Why not say, then, "Let us do evil so that good may come"? Some people, indeed, have insulted me by accusing me of saying this very thing! They will be condemned, as they should be. (Rom 3:8 GNB)

What shall we say then? Shall we continue in sin that grace may abound? Certainly not! How shall we who died to sin live any longer in it? (Rom 6:1-2 NKJV)

What then? Shall we sin because we are not under Law, but under grace? Certainly not! (Rom 6:15 NKJV)

As for you, my friends, you were called to be free. But do not let this freedom become an excuse for letting your physical desires control you. Instead, let love make you serve one another. (Gal 5:13 GNB)

Therefore if Paul, the champion apostle of the New Testament, had to defend the gospel of grace against these accusations and was persecuted by the legalists for preaching this gospel, then we should be considering that perhaps something is wrong if our gospel is *not* making the legalists of our day rise up against us. This is not to say that we should purposely set out to provoke people, but if nobody ever opposes or questions us, it is a sure sign that our beliefs are most likely *not* in line with the truth of the New Covenant.

Law →✝→ Grace

Forgive To Be Forgiven?

At the risk of sounding critical, it remains a sad reality that the Bible Society chose to combine the Old and New Testaments into one single book. This single decision has caused widespread confusion within the ranks of believers throughout the world. Many of the writings in the Bible before the cross portray God to be a harsh, cruel being, set on destroying and punishing people if they dared to disobey the set of moral standards represented by the 10 Commandments and the other laws.

On the contrary, after the cross we see Paul and the other apostles preach a message of unconditional love, grace and mercy to all who place their faith in Christ. In fact, the way that God relates to believers under the New Covenant is so vastly different from the way He treated Israel under the law (remember this was a result of their own doing), that it can't be even remotely compared. The rules of the race have changed, and trying to run according to the old rules while competing in a new race will only cause confusion, condemnation and fear. We'll look at one of these changed rules, namely how God has changed the way He forgives people and what that implies for us.

Without a proper understanding of the context of His words, some of Jesus' statements (before the cross) may seem contrary to what Paul the apostle preached (after the cross).

Jesus said the following:

> And forgive us our debts, as we forgive our debtors. (Matt 6:12 NKJV)

And in another place:

> "And whenever you stand praying, if you have anything against anyone, forgive him, that your Father in heaven may also forgive you

your trespasses. But if you do not forgive, neither will your Father in heaven forgive your trespasses". (Mark 11:25-26 NKJV)

This implies that God's willingness and ability to forgive us is directly related to our ability to forgive others, which means that if we refuse to forgive others, God won't forgive us either. And of course we know that nobody can go to heaven without having their sins forgiven... Take a moment and think about this scenario: It entails that if there is even a single bit of unforgiveness in our hearts, even if it's unintentional, it can condemn us to hell.

On the contrary, Paul made the following statements:

And be kind to one another, tenderhearted, forgiving one another, even as God in Christ forgave you. (Eph 4:32 NKJV, emphasis added)

...bearing with one another, and forgiving one another, if anyone has a complaint against another; even as Christ forgave you, so you also must do. (Col 3:13 NKJV, emphasis added)

The apostle John also added his voice to this chorus, saying:

I write to you, little children, because your sins are forgiven you for His name's sake. (1 John 2:12 NKJV)

The Rules Have Changed

Before the cross (even when Jesus walked the earth), the house of Israel lived under a different set of rules than what we now have. This was called the Old Covenant and it mainly stated that God's faithfulness and His blessings were dependent on Israel's ability to obey all the rules. If they failed (to forgive, to obey, to sacrifice, etc.) they would not be forgiven either and be punished for their transgressions. Jesus also lived under this covenant, which in essence consisted of the laws that were given to Moses and the Israelites.

But when the fullness of the time had come, God sent forth His Son, born of a woman, born under the law. (Gal 4:4 NKJV, emphasis added)

Jesus knew He still had to follow this old set of rules so that He could later offer Himself as the perfect sacrifice for all transgressions and free mankind from the demands of the old rules:

For Christ is the end of the law for righteousness to everyone who believes. (Rom 10:4 NKJV)

But while He was alive (before the cross) *He still had to obey the old rules.*

Our Sins Did Not Survive the Cross

Under the New Covenant God considers those who believe in Him as spotless and blameless in His sight. The writer of Hebrews wrote about how believers would not need the external rules of the law anymore, but would know God's desires in their hearts, having been forgiven all their sins:

> *"This is the covenant that I will make with them after those days, says the LORD: I will put My laws into their hearts, and in their minds I will write them," then He adds, "Their sins and their lawless deeds I will remember no more". (Heb 10:16-17 NKJV)*

> *And you, being dead in your trespasses and the uncircumcision of your flesh, He has made alive together with Him, having forgiven you <u>all</u> trespasses. (Col 2:13 NKJV, emphasis added)*

In the dictionary the word "all" pretty much means what it says: ALL. God has forgiven us *all* our trespasses, which means all past, present *and future* sins. Now most preachers don't have a problem with our past and even our present sins being forgiven, but they have a big problem with someone saying that all our future sins have been forgiven as well, because this implies we've been given a license to sin. However if the Holy Spirit lives inside a person, such a person will not want to indulge in the works of the flesh but strive to live a life worthy of the calling they've been given!

Should We Still Forgive Others Then?

Under the New Covenant we don't need to forgive others in order to receive our own forgiveness anymore, as we've just seen. This however does not make it right to walk in unforgiveness. In the ancient times of the Romans, when a person was murdered, the dead body would literally be tied to the murderer's back with ropes and left to rot. The decomposing flesh would then begin infecting and poisoning the flesh of the living person and the murderer would die a horrible death within a few days.

When we carry around offence in our hearts, it does not affect to a great degree the person who has offended us. It does however eat away at *us* like a cancer, and that's why we *need* to forgive: It's for our own good.

Our last example shows that God took it even a step further: The only difference between a believer and a non-believer is that the believer has placed his faith in God's forgiveness, in other words he's chosen to accept God's free gift of grace.

The unbeliever also stands forgiven, but he has not accepted it yet. *We have to accept a gift before it becomes our own.*

> *...that is, that God was in Christ reconciling <u>the world</u> to Himself, not imputing <u>their</u> trespasses to <u>them</u>, and has committed to <u>us</u> the word of reconciliation. (2 Cor 5:19 NKJV, emphasis added)*

There are two distinct groups in this verse, namely "them" and "us". God through His Son has already reconciled the world ("them") to Himself, which means He's already done everything from His side that mankind will ever need to be saved. All that's left is for believers ("us") to get the good news out to "them" so that when they hear it, they will believe it, *accept* God's forgiveness and be saved.

There is no limit that can be placed on the completeness of God's forgiveness. Each and every dark secret, from the smallest right up to the most hideous act of violence or depravity has already been covered by Jesus' blood. Let's start acting as though we believe we've been forgiven!

Law →✝→ Grace

What is Disobedience?

The answer to this question might surprise many. Most people will say: "Disobedience is doing what God told us *not* to do". Such a response is formulated by trying to relate to God through the law, based on their own level of compliance to the requirements of the 10 Commandments. This will include things like lying, stealing, envy, etc. Some will also say that disobedience is neglecting to do those things which God *did* command us to do. This will include doing good works like giving to the poor, loving our neighbors as ourselves, tithing, etc. However all these things are part of the Old Covenant Law. Yes, even the commandment to "love the Lord your God with all your heart and love you neighbor as yourself" was a quote from an Old Testament Law (Deut 6:5), which has also been entirely fulfilled in Christ. However there is nothing wrong with doing these things, as long as they don't form the basis of how we relate to God. Believers should trust in the finished work of the cross, not in their own performance.

As born again believers we know that we have been redeemed from the curse that comes from disobedience to these laws:

> *Christ has redeemed us from the curse of the law, having become a curse for us. (Gal 3:13 NKJV)*

The law with its requirements that stood opposed to us has been cancelled so that we can be free to love God and live for Him without the fear of judgment:

> *...having wiped out the handwriting of requirements that was against us, which was contrary to us. And He has taken it out of the way, having nailed it to the cross. (Col 2:14 NKJV)*

If there still exists in us any fear of judgment, we have not been made perfect in love yet:

There is no fear in love; but perfect love casts out fear, because fear involves torment. But he who fears has not been made perfect in love. (1 John 4:18 NKJV)

The full wrath and judgment for sin was poured out on Jesus, and God took an oath in Isaiah 54 never to rebuke us or ever be angry with us ever again:

"For this is like the waters of Noah to Me; For as I have sworn that the waters of Noah would no longer cover the earth, so have I sworn that I would not be angry with you, nor rebuke you. (Isa 54:9 NKJV)

Because the law with its requirements was nailed to the cross with Jesus, there is essentially no more law to break anymore.

...because the law brings about wrath; <u>for where there is no law there is no transgression</u>. (Rom 4:15 NKJV, emphasis added)

So what is disobedience then? The following verses are a key:

⁷Therefore, to you who believe, He is precious; <u>but to those who are disobedient</u> "The stone which the builders rejected has become the chief cornerstone," ⁸and "A stone of stumbling and a rock of offense." They [unbelievers] stumble, <u>being disobedient to the word</u>, to which they also were appointed. (1 Pet 2:7-8, annotations and emphasis added)

Verse 7 contrasts two different groups of people very distinctly: Those who believe and those who are *disobedient*. This tells us that those who don't believe are disobedient. The second half of verse 8 also says that they stumble because they are disobedient *to the Word*. What or who is the Word? The Word is Jesus:

In the beginning was the Word, and the Word was with God, and the Word was God. <u>He</u> was in the beginning with God. (John 1:1 & 3 NKJV, emphasis added)

The Word is a person and anybody that doesn't believe in Him stumbles over the stumbling stone and is called "disobedient". Verse 7 also says that to those who believe, He is *precious*. This is because He becomes the author of their salvation, their savior and their brother and they are adopted into His family. What a privilege!

Let's look at another example:

And you He made alive, who <u>were</u> dead in trespasses and sins, in which you once walked according to the course of this world,

> *according to the prince of the power of the air, the spirit who now works in the <u>sons of disobedience</u>. (Eph 2:1-2 NKJV, emphasis added)*

This passage says that we *were* once dead towards God when we still had an old sinful nature, the same nature that still lives on in those who refuse to accept Jesus. They are called the "sons of disobedience". Verse 2 says we "once walked according to the course of this world", which implies we do so no longer.

It's pretty clear from these two verses that being disobedient doesn't really have a lot to do with our deeds. *Being disobedient means not to be saved.* Now with this revelation in mind, let's read these last two verses again. Go on, read them again!

Did the light suddenly go on there? It's amazing how the Holy Spirit illuminates those dark corridors in our minds one by one as we give ourselves to studying God's Word.

The moment we accepted Jesus' perfect sacrifice as the full atonement for our sin, all His obedience was credited to us as a free gift, making us 100% righteous and acceptable to God. Our salvation is now just as secure as Jesus Himself, because we are *in* Christ.

> *But of Him <u>you are in Christ Jesus</u>, who became for us wisdom from God - and righteousness and sanctification and redemption. (1 Cor 1:30 NKJV, emphasis added)*

Because we are now *in* Christ and He lives *in* us, the Father sees His Sons when He looks at us: perfect and without blemish. The only way we could ever lose our right standing with God is if Jesus were to backslide, which of course could never happen.

Law →✝→ Grace

Spirit, Soul and Body

One of the biggest problems that Christians have in understanding how we can be completely righteous (because we don't always "feel" righteous), is the principle of spirit, soul and body. The Bible clearly says we have all three:

> *Now may the God of peace Himself sanctify you completely; and may your whole spirit, soul, and body be preserved blameless at the coming of our Lord Jesus Christ. (1 Thes 5:23 NKJV)*

We *are* a spirit, we *have* a soul, and we live *in* a body. This is very contrary to the worldly belief that we only have a body and mind (remember that mind = soul). Let's briefly look at each one.

<u>The Spirit</u>

When we are born again, our spirit becomes alive to God. Previously our spirit was in a dormant, dead state towards God, but alive to sin (we were *in* sin):

> *...even when we were dead in trespasses, [He] made us alive together with Christ (by grace you have been saved). (Eph 2: 5 NKJV, annotations added)*

But then when we put our faith in Jesus, this old sinful nature was crucified (and buried) with Christ. The Bible calls this sinful nature the "old man":

> *...knowing this, that our <u>old man</u> was crucified with Him, that the body of sin might be done away with, that we should no longer be slaves of sin. (Rom 6:6 NKJV, emphasis added)*

> *For you died, and your life is hidden with Christ in God. (Col 3:3 NKJV)*

This last verse says *"you"* died and through the process of elimination we should easily be able to figure out which part of us it's talking about. Ask yourself: "Did my body die?" The answer of course is "No" because you are still very much alive, reading this book. "Did my soul die?" Again the answer is "No" because at this very moment you are processing the thoughts of what you are reading in this book with your mind, also called your "soul" or "intellect". So since neither the body nor the soul has died, this of course only leaves us with the spirit - this verse is talking about the old sinful spirit man.

The moment we become born again, our spirit becomes alive to God:

> *Now if we died with Christ, we believe that we shall also live with Him* ⁹ *knowing that Christ, having been raised from the dead, dies no more.* ¹⁰ *For the death that He died, He died to sin once for all; but the life that He lives, He lives to God.* ¹¹ *Likewise you also, reckon yourselves to be dead indeed to sin, but alive to God in Christ Jesus our Lord. (Rom 6:8-11 NKJV)*

In verse 11 the word "reckon" actually means "to consider". Compare this paraphrased version of verses 9 to 11 with the verses above:

Verse 9: We know that Christ was raised from the dead and that He cannot die again. Verse 10: He died once on behalf of the whole of mankind, but now He is eternally alive to God. Verse 11: *In the same manner as Christ, consider* yourself also to be dead to sin, because just like Christ you *are* dead to sin! And just like Christ is now alive to God, consider yourself also to be *alive to God*!

And here is the most amazing part: At the moment of salvation our born again spirit is created just as righteous as Jesus, perfectly holy and glorious and has the very nature of Jesus Christ Himself! The Father made Jesus to be sin in our place so we could receive His righteousness as a free gift!

> *For He made Him who knew no sin to be sin for us, that we might become the righteousness of God in Him. (2 Cor 5:21 NKJV)*

Our born again spirit is sometimes also called the "new man" or "inward man". The last part of Ephesians 4 talks about our behavior towards other people and verse 24 says that just as our inner man *has already been* created according to the very image of Jesus, we should now also let our actions reflect this change that has occurred inside us:

> *...and that you put on the new man which <u>was</u> created according to God, in true righteousness and holiness. (Eph 4:24 NKJV, emphasis added)*

> *And <u>have</u> put on the new man, which is renewed in knowledge after the image of him that created him. (Col 3:10 NKJV, emphasis added)*

This born again spirit man inside us can never change; it is made righteous for ever! It is actually "fused" together with the Holy Spirit Himself!

> *But he who is joined to the Lord is one spirit with Him. (1 Cor 6:17 NKJV)*

This means that if we were ever able to corrupt *our* spirit, we would also be able to corrupt the Holy Spirit because we have been joined to Him and they are one Spirit. And of course we know this can never happen. It is a one way stream: The Holy Spirit (or our born again Spirit) can never be manipulated negatively, it can only emanate goodness. This goodness can however be choked-up, which is called "quenching" the Spirit (1 Thessalonians 5:19).

<u>The Soul</u>

This is the realm of the psyche and includes the mind, will, intellect, personality and emotions. This part does not instantly change when we are born again. Yes we've now made a choice for Christ to follow Him and serve Him, but this part of us still has the old thought patterns and habits of our BC (before Christ) days. These habits may have been formed out of mere self preservation instincts, or by us yielding our members to the lustful desires of our old sinful nature.

Even though we don't want to sin anymore, we still find that our behavior does not always line up with what we *want* to do. This is what Paul talks about in Romans 7:

> *For what I am doing, I do not understand. For what I will to do, that I do not practice; but what I hate, that I do. Now if I do what I will not to do, it is no longer I who do it, but sin that dwells in me. For I delight in the law of God according to the inward man. But I see another law in my members, warring against the law of my mind, and bringing me into captivity to the law of sin which is in my members. (Rom 7:15, 20, 22-23 NKJV)*

Our soul / mind is the part of us that we spend the rest of our life renewing. We need to train our mind to agree with what already happened in our spirit. How do we do this? Well, truth doesn't just automatically jump out at us while we sit and do nothing. Jesus said that "the truth will set you free", but it is only the truth that we *know* that will set us free. By devoting quality time to God, studying the word, praying, spending time with fellow believers, etc. we get to behold the beauty of our Father and have our minds washed with truth.

> *And do not be conformed to this world, but be transformed by the renewing of your mind, that you may prove what is that good and acceptable and perfect will of God. (Rom 12:2 NKJV)*

A desire for intimacy will prompt us into *wanting* to do these things. The Spirit of God inside us cries out to the Father, deep calling to deep, wanting to romance and woo us. The above list of things to do is not a recipe or a list of "have to's". The need to study the word, pray, etc. will manifest itself as a desire in us, the mighty Holy Spirit expressing His desire to lead us into all truth (John 16:13).

This is also why we are told to set our minds on the things above (Colossians 3:2), because the more we think God's thoughts, the faster our minds will be transformed. As our old sinful thought patterns begin to starve, the mind will come more and more into agreement with our born again spirit.

The Body

When Jesus died, He redeemed us through His blood. At that moment the believer's spirit becomes alive towards God and their body a temple of the Holy Spirit.

> *Or do you not know that your body is the temple of the Holy Spirit who is in you, whom you have from God, and you are not your own? For you were bought at a price; therefore glorify God in your body and in your spirit, which are God's. (1 Cor 6:19-20 NKJV)*

Our body will follow either the spirit or the mind, depending which one we give control to. If we give our mind control (and our mind has not yet been renewed), we are walking according the flesh and the fruit of this is death - death in the form of us reaping the results of our ungodly actions.

> *What benefit did you reap at that time from the things you are now ashamed of? Those things result in death! (Rom 6:21 NKJV)*

Note that even though we might sometimes reap earthly consequences for our actions, God will never punish us for our mistakes since *all* mankind's sin was punished in the body of Christ.

But now, since we have been made alive *in* the spirit (born again), let us walk according to the spirit! If our old sinful nature has been crucified with Christ, why would we still want to live according to it? As our mind becomes more and more renewed, our body and mind / soul will also walk more and more in line with what has already happened in our spirit, becoming more committed to the righteous purposes of God.

> *Just as you used to offer the parts of your body in slavery to impurity and to ever-increasing wickedness, so now offer them in slavery to righteousness leading to holiness. (Rom 6:19 NKJV)*

> *I say then: Walk in the Spirit, and you shall not fulfill the lust of the flesh. For the flesh lusts against the Spirit, and the Spirit against the flesh; and these are contrary to one another, so that you do not do the things that you wish. (Gal 5:16-17 NKJV)*

Remember that a believer *is* a spirit; they *have* a soul and *live* in a body. Their spirit is completely righteous and holy and since the believer *is* a spirit, the actual person has been made the righteousness of God! It's now simply a matter of getting our mind and body to line up with this truth.

Law →✝→ Grace

Righteousness Through the Law Pt 1

As more and more Christians realize there is a revolution in the earth for the church to be released from the captivity of legalism and law, the people that are still preaching the law are also becoming more ferocious than ever! By reading through the websites of these ministries on the internet it is clear that they are becoming more and more divisive; more determined to steal from believers the liberty for which Jesus paid such a high price and also more clever in their arguments, even trying to seduce and recapture those who for long periods have been soaring in the currents of grace.

Churches are "warning" their people against being "deceived" by grace preachers, cautioning them that grace can't be preached alone, but should be understood in the context of the whole Bible. They preach that grace by itself can apparently lead to a false understanding of what God had intended with the cross; the right thing to do would be to mix a healthy dose of law in there as well to "balance" the message. Nothing could be further from the truth!

It is these preachers of law that love to quote scriptures from the gospels of Matthew, Mark, Luke and John out of context, forgetting that the crowds who Jesus was preaching to were Jews! These Jews had been polluted with hundreds of years of preaching of the Old Testament Law, hearing day after day that it is their obedience to the law will cause them to become righteous and that their level of morality and good performance will earn them God's acceptance and blessings.

God never originally meant for us to try to relate to Him in this way! Just after God's commands were written on stone and He set the choice of curse (for disobedience) or blessing (for obedience) before Israel, He said this to Moses:

> And the LORD said to Moses: "Behold, you will rest with your
> fathers; and this people will rise and play the harlot with the gods

> *of the foreigners of the land, where they go to be among them, and they will forsake Me and break My covenant which I have made with them. (Deut 31:16 NKJV)*

God knew that Israel would not be able to keep His laws and commands, but because Israel refused to have a personal relationship with God (always asking Moses to speak to God on their behalf) and despite all the many miracles God did when leading them out of Egypt (showing great patience with Israel despite all their continuous murmuring and complaining in the desert), they persisted in their unbelief in God, not trusting that He could and *would* lead them to the Promised Land. They were self righteous and "stiff nicked" as God called them:

> *Go up to a land flowing with milk and honey; for I will not go up in your midst, lest I consume you on the way, for you are a stiff-necked people. (Ex 33:3 NKJV)*

Moses also said to them, as they were about to cross the Jordan River:

> *Therefore understand that the LORD your God is not giving you this good land to possess because of your righteousness, for you are a stiff-necked people. (Deut 6:9 NKJV)*

Now imagine centuries of "stiff necked-ness" later and we would have an idea of the crowd that Jesus was preaching into.

Another interesting fact is that God had never appointed any Pharisees, Sadducees or Scribes anywhere in the Bible, but only priests to minister in the temple. The Babylonian Empire of king Nebuchadnezzar overthrew the Jewish kingdom in the year 586 BC and had thousands of Israelites exiled to Babylon. After the overthrow of Babylonia by the Persian Empire, the Persian ruler (Cyrus the Great) gave Jews permission to return to their homeland in 538BC and to rebuild their temple.

The parties of the Pharisees and their opponents, the Sadducees, were two of the earliest sects to emerge in the Second Temple Period. In general, whereas the Sadducees were conservative, aristocratic monarchists, the Pharisees were eclectic, popular and more democratic.

These sects also forsook many of God's laws and replaced them with manmade rules and codes, which resulted in what is traditionally known today as Judaism[1]. Jesus rebuked them time and again for replacing God's commandments with manmade traditions. Look for example how they tried to corner Jesus, saying his disciples transgressed the *tradition* of the elders:

> *Then the scribes and Pharisees who were from Jerusalem came to Jesus, saying, "Why do Your disciples transgress the tradition of the elders? For they do not wash their hands when they eat bread." He answered and said to them, "Why do you also transgress the commandment of God because of your tradition? For God commanded, saying, 'Honor your father and your mother'; and, 'He who curses father or mother, let him be put to death.' But you say, 'Whoever says to his father or mother, "Whatever profit you might have received from me is a gift to God" – then he need not honor his father or mother.' Thus you have made the commandment of God of no effect by your tradition. Hypocrites! Well did Isaiah prophesy about you, saying: 'These people draw near to Me with their mouth, and honor Me with their lips, but their heart is far from Me. And in vain they worship Me, teaching as doctrines the commandments of men'. (Matt 15:1-9 NKJV)*

The Jews had over the centuries reduced the perfect law of God to a standard that could be "kept", but Jesus wanted to show them that *everybody* falls short. Even if some claimed they had kept the law their whole life, Jesus pointed out they still lacked in some other area. He wanted people to see that only by putting our faith in a Savior (Him), could we ever be restored unto God and by faith obtain grace, mercy and justification. Paul later received this revelation from God and wrote the following:

> *But now the righteousness of God apart from the law is revealed, being witnessed by the Law and the Prophets, even the righteousness of God, through faith in Jesus Christ, to all and on all who believe. For there is no difference; <u>for all have sinned and fall short of the glory of God</u>* [no matter how well they may think they have been keeping the laws], *being justified freely by His grace through the redemption that is in Christ Jesus. (Rom 3:21-24 NKJV, annotations and emphasis added)*

> *Therefore we conclude that a man is justified by faith apart from the deeds of the law. (Rom 3:28 NKJV)*

Verse 23 in the above passage is a favorite with preachers of the law, but they never read it in conjunction with the very next verse, which says that even though everybody on the planet has sinned and fallen short of God's glory, they are justified freely by their faith in Christ. We'll look at this verse again in the next chapter.

The Context of Jesus' Words

If we read Jesus' teachings through this perspective (namely that He was trying to show people they could never measure up to the standard of the law in their own efforts) we can see why He always got so angry at the Pharisees who thought that God would accept them by their "holy" living and why He also showed such mercy and love to those who simply believed in Him and knew they couldn't make it without Him.

The law will always point out our mistakes, make us feel guilty and show us that we haven't done enough. When the rich young ruler boasted in his own morality, claiming he had kept all the laws since he was a young boy, Jesus showed him that he *still* fell short: he valued money more than heavenly treasures.

> *A certain ruler asked him, "Good Teacher, what must I do to inherit eternal life?" So Jesus said to him, "Why do you call Me good? No one is good but One, that is, God. You know the commandments: 'Do not commit adultery,' 'Do not murder,' 'Do not steal,' 'Do not bear false witness,' 'Honor your father and your mother.'" And he said, "All these things I have kept from my youth." So when Jesus heard these things, He said to him, "You still lack one thing. Sell all that you have and distribute to the poor, and you will have treasure in Heaven; and come, follow Me." But when he heard this, he became very sorrowful, for he was very rich. (Luk 18:18-23 NKJV)*

But now the modern day "law preachers" will take this scripture and tell God's precious children (who have been freed from the law) that it is wrong for Christians to have lots of money and that you can't go to heaven if you are rich.

Be careful of those who demand a standard of holy living to gain God's approval or who put a disclaimer on God's blessings. We live under a New Covenant and the law (with all its demands of "right living") has been crucified with Christ:

> *And you, being dead in your trespasses and the uncircumcision of your flesh, He has made alive together with Him, having forgiven you all trespasses, having wiped out the handwriting of requirements that was against us, which was contrary to us. And He has taken it out of the way, having nailed it to the cross. (Col 2:13-14 NKJV)*

Remember the 10 Commandments which were engraved on stones tablets?

> *But if the ministry of death, written and engraved on stones... (2 Cor 3:7a NKJV)*

The 10 Commandments is called the ministry of death!

> *...but our sufficiency is from God, who also made us sufficient as ministers of the new covenant, not of the letter but of the Spirit; for the letter kills, but the Spirit gives life. (2 Cor 3:5b-6 NKJV)*

This says the letter (the law) kills!

Therefore let us continue to contend for the freedom which we have been called into: the glorious liberty of the New Covenant! Let us beware of the modern day Pharisees who with their form of godliness (void of power) try to snare us into being performance driven, legalistic and continuously under pressure to try and live up to some expired standard.

> *Stand fast therefore in the liberty by which Christ has made us free, and do not be entangled again with a yoke of bondage. (Gal 5:1 NKJV)*

Law →✝→ Grace

Righteousness Through the Law Pt 2

It's quite amazing how some modern day preachers want to put on God's children the laws and regulations of the Old Covenant which they themselves cannot fulfill, nor the Israelites (Jews) could manage to live by for hundreds of years. When certain Jews came to Antioch, the apostle Peter withdrew himself and did not eat with the Gentile believers as this was considered a sin by those who still lived according to the law. But Paul rebuked him and the other Jews who joined him in his hypocrisy:

> But when I saw that they were not straightforward about the truth of the gospel, I said to Peter before them all, "If you, being a Jew, live in the manner of Gentiles and not as the Jews, why do you compel Gentiles to live as Jews? (Gal 2:14 NKJV)

A similar thing happened in the churches of Galatia. The Galatian Christians didn't renounce Jesus as being their Messiah, but legalistic Jews had convinced them that they couldn't be right with God by *only* believing in what Jesus had done. They were being told they also had to keep the Old Testament Law in order for God to accept them. The same lie is being propagated today and church congregations are being manipulated to perform according to manmade standards, else the Lord won't accept them, answer their prayers or bless them. Lots of people love to quote the Old Covenant scripture Leviticus 11: 44-45 out of context, where God tells Israel: "Be Holy, for I am holy". It's logical that living a holy lifestyle is not a bad thing, but when we do this in order to gain God's approval, it is not the gospel.

Manmade Laws

In Paul's day, the issue was circumcision. The legalistic believers still held fast that people had to be circumcised in accordance with the Law of Moses in order

45

to be accepted by God. Today the same legalistic message is being preached using different tactics. Nowadays people are made to feel guilty by using things like prayer, Bible study, church attendance and other actions of "right living" as necessary requirements for God to love and accept them. Instead people should actually be told over and over again that their faith in what Christ did for them is more than enough!

> *Therefore we conclude that a man is justified by faith apart from the deeds of the law. (Rom 3:28 NKJV)*

It is not a combination of what Jesus did for us *plus* our own actions of holiness: Jesus plus anything equals nothing. Jesus plus nothing equals everything.

No one argues that we shouldn't pray, study the Word, go to church, etc, but any time it is argued that God is angry with us if we fail to do these things, it's not the true gospel. That type of teaching puts the burden of salvation on us and opens us to condemnation and attacks from the devil. This is what Paul called a perversion of the gospel:

> *I marvel that you are turning away so soon from Him who called you in the grace of Christ, to a different gospel, which is not another; but there are some who trouble you and want to pervert the gospel of Christ. (Gal 1: 6-7 NKJV)*

Not Even a Little Bit of Law!

A person who claims that others must adhere to even one regulation stated in the Old Covenant Law is bound by the whole law:

> *And I testify again to every man who becomes circumcised* [a stipulation of one of the laws] *that he is a debtor to keep the whole law. (Gal 5:3 NKJV, annotations added)*

Someone cannot just choose to adhere to one (or some) law and not adhere strictly to all the others, as this would literally demonstrate Pharisaic hypocrisy. But by simply putting our faith in Jesus who obeyed all the laws on our behalf, our sin (sinful condition) is imputed (carried over or given) to Him and His righteousness is given to us as a free gift!

Romans 3:23

Many people also love to quote Romans 3:23 out of context to try and make God's children feel guilty and conscious of their mistakes:

...for all have sinned and fall short of the glory of God. (Rom 3:23 NKJV)

But this verse seems quite different when it's actually read it in the context of the verses around it. Let's read from verse 21 to 24:

> *²¹ But now the righteousness of God <u>apart from the law</u> is revealed, being witnessed by the Law and the Prophets, ²² even the righteousness of God, through faith in Jesus Christ, <u>to all and on all who believe</u>. For there is no difference; ²³ for all have sinned and fall short of the glory of God, ²⁴ <u>being justified freely by His grace</u> through the redemption that is in Christ Jesus. (Rom 3:21-24 NKJV, emphasis added)*

This means that now the Father doesn't just see us as if we had never sinned, He sees us as if we had also obeyed all the laws our entire life! Jesus took upon Himself what we deserved (our punishment) and gave as a free gift to us what He deserved (the Father's approval and blessings for 100% complete obedience). Now that's a pretty good deal, hallelujah!

Below is a paraphrased version of Romans 3:21-24 (compare it to the original verses above). May the joy and jubilation of a soul set at liberty flood anybody that reads this. Praise God for the FREE GIFT of righteousness!

> *²¹ But one day in the "court" of Heaven, the Law and the Prophets will stand up; point their finger to every person who has believed in Jesus and say: "That person is righteous! ²² By putting their faith in Jesus, everyone that believes is given the same righteousness as God!" ²³ For although they were once called "sinners" and fell short of the glory of God, ²⁴ they were justified freely by His grace through the redemption that is in Christ Jesus. (Rom 3:21-24, author's paraphrased version)*

Amen.

Law →✝→ Grace

First Adam and Last Adam

God created Adam perfectly in His own image, without sin or blemish. However through Adam's disobedience in the Garden of Eden, he died spiritually and became sinful by nature. The glory of God which had covered him up to that point lifted off him and he became aware of his nakedness (lack of glory). And since the seed of the entire human race was still inside Adam, every person born after him would inherit this sinful nature at birth. Therefore through the sin of one man, death came into the world.

> *Therefore, just as through one man sin entered the world, and death through sin, and thus death spread to all men... (Rom 5:12a NKJV)*

The result is that when every human being is born, they are born into this inherent sinful state (with a sinful nature). Without asking for it, sin is automatically imparted to us at birth because of first Adam's sin. **Thus when we are born, we are born into first Adam.**

But when we come into Christ (last Adam) by simply putting our faith in Him, His righteousness is automatically imputed to us as a free gift. We are restored to first Adam's original spiritual state of being blameless, justified and glorified. On the inside we actually look exactly the same as Jesus; we are conformed to the image of God's own Son!

> *For whom He foreknew, He also predestined to be conformed to the image of His Son, that He might be the firstborn among many brethren. Moreover whom He predestined, these He also called; whom He called, these He also justified; and whom He justified, these He also glorified. (Rom 8:29-30 NKJV)*

Thus when we are born again, we are born into last Adam.

First Adam, a Pattern of Last Adam

When a human being is born, they receive a sinful nature without asking for it or deserving it. Therefore if anybody on the earth were to perish when they die, they would technically not do so because of something they did wrong - they would perish because of first Adam's sin and the sinful nature they inherited from him as a free gift.

By the same token, whenever somebody is born again, they receive another, much greater free gift, namely the righteousness of God. And again the fact that they would go to heaven is not due to anything they did right, but because of what Christ did right on their behalf. We see therefore that neither the sinful nor the righteous natures can be earned or deserved. The one is given by first Adam and the other by last Adam.

> *For if by the one man's offense death reigned through the one [first Adam], much more those who receive abundance of grace and of the gift of righteousness will reign in life through the One, Jesus Christ [last Adam]. Therefore, as through one man's offense judgment came to all men, resulting in condemnation, even so through one Man's righteous act the free gift came to all men, resulting in justification of life. For as by one man's disobedience many were made sinners, so also by one Man's obedience many will be made righteous. (Rom 5:17-19 NKJV, annotations added)*

In 1 Corinthians 15 we see Paul addressing this issue again:

> *For since by man came death, by Man also came the resurrection of the dead. For as in Adam all die, even so in Christ all shall be made alive. (1 Cor 15:21-22 NKJV)*

Because mankind's spiritual life and authority was initially surrendered to the devil by a man, Christ also had to come to the earth in the form of a man to take it back again from the devil, see 1 Corinthians 15:21 (above) again. Later in the same chapter Paul continues to portray Christ's ability to impart life:

> *And so it is written, "The first man Adam became a living being." The last Adam became a life-giving spirit. (1 Cor 15:45 NKJV)*

A.W. Tozer wrote the following: *"What we need to restore power to the Christian testimony is not soft talk about brotherhood, but an honest recognition that two human races occupy the earth simultaneously: a fallen race that sprang from the loins of Adam and a regenerate race that is born of the Spirit through the redemption which is in Christ Jesus."*

Now carefully consider the following two statements:

1. No amount of holy living or law keeping could move us out of our fallen state in first Adam. We were stuck there and the only way to be saved was to put our faith in Jesus Christ (Romans 10:9-10).

2. Likewise, the moment we come into last Adam (Jesus Christ), no amount of bad behavior or "unholy" living can move us out of this position of perfect righteousness.

Although most Christians believe the first statement to be true, they have somewhat of a problem believing the second. The first thought that comes into many people's minds when reading the second statement is this: "This guy is saying that I can just go out and do whatever I want!" This is mainly due to the fact that people don't understand the power of the New Creation yet and don't have a revelation of what a person is actually turned into when they are born again. When the Holy Spirit lives inside a person, such a person does not *want* to sin – they actually *want* to serve God, to live an upright life as an example to others and to love their neighbor, because this is the desire of the Holy Spirit within them. So in essence we *can* actually go out and do whatever we want, because if the Holy Spirit is really living inside us we will *want* to do good!

Another reason why most people find the second statement (above) so hard to believe is because we forget that God does not relate to us based on our own level of obedience anymore. God is a spirit and since we are also spiritual beings He relates to us (blesses us, loves us, provides for us) based on our spiritual status, not according to our physical behavior. And since our spirits have been for ever made righteous, God is for ever pleased with us regardless of our behavior. God sees the perfect obedience of His beloved Son whenever He looks at us and remembers how He fully defeated sin through Jesus' death on the cross.

God does not count *any* of our sins (past, present or future) against us. He is not surprised when we sin. He is not shocked by the ungodliness going on in the world today. God is perfectly content, at rest and at peace, all the time enveloped in the amazing love of the Trinity (imagine the amazing love between the Father, Son and Holy Spirit!). God is secure in Himself, secure in His bride and secure in us, His children. He does not count our sin against us – He already had the rod of His punishment broken on the back of Jesus. God established everlasting peace between Himself and mankind:

> *Therefore, having been justified by faith, we have peace with God through our Lord Jesus Christ. (Rom 5:1 NKJV)*

Why then do we still try to justify ourselves by working so hard to gain God's acceptance?

*But to him who does not work but believes on Him who justifies
the ungodly, his faith is accounted for righteousness, just as David
also describes the blessedness of the man to whom God imputes
righteousness apart from works: "Blessed are those whose lawless
deeds are forgiven, and whose sins are covered; Blessed is the man
to whom the LORD shall not impute sin". (Rom 4:5-8 NKJV)*

Our sin was imputed (accounted) to Jesus, so we can rest in our Father's love, knowing that God will never count our sins (past, present and future) against us anymore!

Law →✝→ Grace

Nullification of the Law

From the time of Adam and Eve until the time when the law was given to Moses and the Israelites, there was no law in the world. God treated all those *who believed in Him* with love and grace, regardless of their obedience or disobedience. Mankind did however still suffer the consequences of their own actions, because the law of death reigned in the world:

> *Nevertheless death reigned from Adam to Moses, even over those who had not sinned according to the likeness of the transgression of Adam, who is a type of Him who was to come. (Rom 5:14 NKJV)*

The main difference between this period and the period *after* the law had been given, was that God did not punish people for their sins back then.

But what about Adam and Eve who were chased out of the Garden after they had eaten from the Tree of the Knowledge of Good and Evil? In this instance God was actually protecting Adam and Eve, because if they had continued to stay in the Garden and eaten from the Tree of Life as well, they would have continued to live forever, but in an everlasting state of sinfulness!

Abraham Not Under the Law

In Abraham's time the nation of Israel did not yet even exist – remember Abraham was the father of Isaac, who was the father of Jacob, who later became known as Israel.

> *God said to him, "Your name is Jacob, but you will no longer be called Jacob; your name will be Israel." So he named him Israel. (Gen 35:10 NKJV)*

52

Israel had twelve sons who became the fathers of the twelve tribes of Israel. And to these twelve tribes God gave the law, but only 430 years after Abraham lived:

> *Now to Abraham and his Seed were the promises made. He does not say, "And to seeds," as of many, but as of one, "And to your Seed," who is Christ. And this I say, that <u>the law, which was four hundred and thirty years later,</u> cannot annul the covenant that was confirmed before by God in Christ, that it should make the promise of no effect. (Gal 3:16-17 NKJV, emphasis added)*

Let's look at a few more examples of how God treated people *before* the law was given:

After Cain killed his brother Abel, God *still* put a mark on Cain to prevent anybody from killing him and God even said that if anybody tried to kill Cain, that Cain would be avenged seven fold! Cain's actions caused him to be cursed *from the earth*:

> *So now you are cursed from the earth, which has opened its mouth to receive your brother's blood from your hand. (Gen 4:11 NKJV)*

Perhaps he was even hated by people, *but he wasn't cursed by God*. Look again: he was cursed from the EARTH. God still loved him the same.

In Genesis 12 Abraham lied to Pharaoh about his wife Sarah to save his own neck because he thought that the Egyptians would kill him due to the fact that Sarah was a very beautiful woman. Here we see that even though Abraham was clearly in the wrong, God rebuked the Pharaoh! And what's even more, afterwards Abraham left Egypt laden with slaves and cattle and wealth! So Abraham lied but became rich. Does this look like God was punishing him?

How Israel Landed Up in Egypt

So how did Israel end up in Egypt? Joseph was betrayed by his brothers who sold him to slave dealers and he was taken to Egypt. He later interpreted the Pharaoh's dreams and was appointed to the highest position in the whole of Egypt, except for Pharaoh himself. The whole region suffered an extreme famine and Joseph's eleven brothers and their father (Jacob) came to live with him in Egypt.

> *So Joseph dwelt in Egypt, he and his father's household. And Joseph lived one hundred and ten years. (Gen 50:22 NKJV)*

And that's how the twelve tribes of Israel came to be in Egypt. They then began to multiply exceedingly because God was with them. And after a couple of hundred years we see the following:

> *And Joseph died, all his brothers, and all that generation. But the children of Israel were fruitful and increased abundantly, multiplied and grew exceedingly mighty; and the land was filled with them. Now there arose a new king over Egypt, who did not know Joseph. And he said to his people, "Look, the people of the children of Israel are more and mightier than we; come, let us deal shrewdly with them, lest they multiply, and it happen, in the event of war, that they also join our enemies and fight against us, and so go up out of the land." Therefore they set taskmasters over them to afflict them with their burdens. And they built for Pharaoh supply cities, Pithom and Raamses. But the more they afflicted them, the more they multiplied and grew. And they were in dread of the children of Israel. So the Egyptians made the children of Israel serve with rigor. (Ex 1:6-13 NKJV)*

Israel in the Desert

We can follow this thread of God's grace to those who believed in Him, right up to the time where the law was given (Exodus 19-20). Despite Israel's murmuring and complaining in the desert, God always provided for them (manna, water out of a rock, a pillar of fire, etc). He never punished nor killed even one single person that believed in Him. But after Israel had received the law, we see a drastic change. They now had to obey its requirements perfectly in order to be blessed and accepted by God, for they now had to relate to God on the basis of their own level of obedience to the law. If they failed to hold up their end of the bargain, God could not fail to hold up His end (by punishing them) because that would make Him a liar.

Israel were the ones who *agreed* to this covenant and said in their pride that they would obey *all* that God commanded them to do, as if they were ever going to manage that!

> *And if we are careful to obey all this law before the Lord our God, as he has commanded us, that will be our righteousness. (Deut 6:25 NIV, emphasis added).*

They were trusting that their own righteousness would be good enough to measure up to the standards of the law, but sadly through history the story of Israel's demise has been clear for all the world to see, as they have fallen short of the standards of the law again and again. Let's now take an in depth look at what the consequences are of trying to live under the law. We'll look at several examples of how Israel came up short of its requirements and the dire results it had for them. This might also help to shed some light as to how a loving, kind God can punish and almost destroy an entire nation – and it must have ripped His loving heart apart...

Blessings and Curses

One of the most shocking chapters of the Bible is Deuteronomy 28, where God gave Israel the promises of blessing for obedience or of curse for disobedience. Israel would receive the promises of blessing only if they obeyed ALL God's commandments. Remember it was not only just the 10 Commandments but also the 613 commandments and principles of law and ethics contained in the Torah or Five Books of Moses. That meant that Israel had to keep *all* these commandments if they wanted to be blessed by God and the same goes for any person today that expects God to bless them on the basis of obeying the law - it's not just the 10 Commandments but *all* these other laws as well. Let's look at the first 14 verses of the chapter, which stipulates the blessings they would receive for obedience:

> *"Now it shall come to pass, if you diligently obey the voice of the LORD your God, to observe carefully all His commandments which I command you today, that the LORD your God will set you high above all nations of the earth. And all these blessings shall come upon you and overtake you, because you obey the voice of the LORD your God: "Blessed shall you be in the city, and blessed shall you be in the country. "Blessed shall be the fruit of your body, the produce of your ground and the increase of your herds, the increase of your cattle and the offspring of your flocks. "Blessed shall be your basket and your kneading bowl. "Blessed shall you be when you come in, and blessed shall you be when you go out. "The LORD will cause your enemies who rise against you to be defeated before your face; they shall come out against you one way and flee before you seven ways. "The LORD will command the blessing on you in your storehouses and in all to which you set your hand, and He will bless you in the land which the LORD your God is giving you. "The LORD will establish you as a holy people to Himself, just as He has sworn to you, if you keep the commandments of the LORD your God and walk in His ways. Then all peoples of the earth shall see that you are called by the name of the LORD, and they shall be afraid of you. And the LORD will grant you plenty of goods, in the fruit of your body, in the increase of your livestock, and in the produce of your ground, in the land of which the LORD swore*

to your fathers to give you. The LORD will open to you His good treasure, the Heavens, to give the rain to your land in its season, and to bless all the work of your hand. You shall lend to many nations, but you shall not borrow. And the LORD will make you the head and not the tail; you shall be above only, and not be beneath, if you heed the commandments of the LORD your God, which I command you today, and are careful to observe them. So you shall not turn aside from any of the words which I command you this day, to the right or the left, to go after other gods to serve them. (Deut 28:1-14 NKJV)

And then in Deuteronomy 28:15-68 God set before them the curses for disobedience, which are too numerous to list here. Now right there a warning light should have begun to flicker to Israel: This covenant had only 15 verses of blessings but it had 52 verses of curses! Something wasn't right! Doesn't this serve as even more proof that this covenant was an inferior covenant and not God's best plan for mankind? No right minded person would have agreed to the conditions of this agreement if they had thought about it properly. Remember that the curses for disobedience were to befall them if they disobeyed *any* of the 613 commandments of the Mosaic Law! The "Mosaic" Law was derived from "Moses" who was Israel's chosen leader at the time.

Too many people who still choose to live according to the Old Covenant Law today have very conveniently decided that they can choose which commandments they want to obey and which ones they don't like. The trend is to write off the parts of the law, which according to these people, are not applicable because they are merely ceremonies and rituals. However the Bible tells us that the law is a composite unity:

For whoever shall keep the whole law, and yet stumble in one point, he is guilty of all. (Jam 2:10 NKJV)

The Bible is a shockingly visual book in certain parts, but we often prefer to skip to the parts that we like or that we're most familiar with. Take a deep breath as we read about a few of the consequences that Israel had to face if they failed in *one single* aspect of the law:

"But it shall come to pass, if you do not obey the voice of the LORD your God, to observe carefully all His commandments and His statutes which I command you today, that all these curses will come upon you and overtake you: (Deut 28:15 NKJV)

"The LORD will send on you cursing, confusion, and rebuke in all that you set your hand to do, until you are destroyed and until

you perish quickly, because of the wickedness of your doings in which you have forsaken Me. The LORD will make the plague cling to you until He has consumed you from the land which you are going to possess. The LORD will strike you with consumption, with fever, with inflammation, with severe burning fever, with the sword, with scorching, and with mildew; they shall pursue you until you perish. And your Heavens which are over your head shall be bronze, and the earth which is under you shall be iron. The LORD will change the rain of your land to powder and dust; from the Heaven it shall come down on you until you are destroyed. (Deut 28:16, 21-24 NKJV)

Your carcasses shall be food for all the birds of the air and the beasts of the earth, and no one shall frighten them away. The LORD will strike you with the boils of Egypt, with tumors, with the scab, and with the itch, from which you cannot be healed. The LORD will strike you with madness and blindness and confusion of heart. And you shall grope at noonday, as a blind man gropes in darkness; you shall not prosper in your ways; you shall be only oppressed and plundered continually, and no one shall save you. "You shall betroth a wife, but another man shall lie with her; you shall build a house, but you shall not dwell in it; you shall plant a vineyard, but shall not gather its grapes. (Deut 28:26-30 NKJV)

Remember how Israel was carried away in captivity by their enemies? Ever wondered why God allowed this to happen? Because they had a covenant with Him and when they didn't uphold their part, God still had to uphold His part because He cannot be unfaithful:

Your sons and your daughters shall be given to another people, and your eyes shall look and fail with longing for them all day long; and there shall be no strength in your hand. A nation whom you have not known shall eat the fruit of your land and the produce of your labor, and you shall be only oppressed and crushed continually. So you shall be driven mad because of the sight which your eyes see. The LORD will strike you in the knees and on the legs with severe boils which cannot be healed, and from the sole of your foot to the top of your head. "The LORD will bring you and the king whom you set over you to a nation which neither you nor your fathers have known, and there you shall serve other gods—wood and stone. And you shall become an astonishment, a proverb, and a byword among all nations where the LORD will drive you. You shall beget sons and daughters, but they shall not be yours; for they shall go into captivity. Therefore you shall serve your enemies, whom the LORD

> *will send against you, in hunger, in thirst, in nakedness, and in*
> *need of everything; and He will put a yoke of iron on your neck*
> *until He has destroyed you. (Deut 28:32-37, 41, 48 NKJV)*

Plagues in the Desert

So let's go back to Israel in the desert, after God had given them the law. Because of their failure to hold up their end of the covenant, God started sending plagues and calamities upon them, because He had to remain faithful to His side of the agreement due to the fact that He cannot lie. Let's read about a few of these plagues.

Under the Old Covenant Law, God had appointed Aaron and the Levites as the only people who were allowed to minister to Him. Now certain men rose up against them and Moses, claiming that they too had the right to be priests, thereby breaking the law:

> *Now Korah the son of Izhar, the son of Kohath, the son of Levi,*
> *with Dathan and Abiram the sons of Eliab, and On the son of*
> *Peleth, sons of Reuben, took men; and they rose up before Moses*
> *with some of the children of Israel, two hundred and fifty leaders*
> *of the congregation, representatives of the congregation, men of*
> *renown. They gathered together against Moses and Aaron, and*
> *said to them, "You take too much upon yourselves, for all the*
> *congregation is holy, every one of them, and the LORD is among*
> *them. Why then do you exalt yourselves above the assembly of the*
> *LORD?" So when Moses heard it, he fell on his face; and he spoke*
> *to Korah and all his company, saying, "Tomorrow morning the*
> *LORD will show who is His and who is holy, and will cause him*
> *to come near to Him. That one whom He chooses He will cause*
> *to come near to Him. Do this: Take censers, Korah and all your*
> *company; put fire in them and put incense in them before the*
> *LORD tomorrow, and it shall be that the man whom the LORD*
> *chooses is the holy one. You take too much upon yourselves, you sons*
> *of Levi!" Then Moses said to Korah, "Hear now, you sons of Levi:*
> *Is it a small thing to you that the God of Israel has separated you*
> *from the congregation of Israel, to bring you near to Himself, to*
> *do the work of the tabernacle of the LORD, and to stand before*
> *the congregation to serve them; and that He has brought you near*
> *to Himself, you and all your brethren, the sons of Levi, with you?*
> *And are you seeking the priesthood also? Therefore you and all*
> *your company are gathered together against the LORD. And what*
> *is Aaron that you complain against him?" And Moses sent to call*

> *Dathan and Abiram the sons of Eliab, but they said, "We will not come up! Is it a small thing that you have brought us up out of a land flowing with milk and honey, to kill us in the wilderness, that you should keep acting like a prince over us? Moreover you have not brought us into a land flowing with milk and honey, nor given us inheritance of fields and vineyards. Will you put out the eyes of these men? We will not come up!" (Num 16:1-14 NKJV)*

Then the next day 250 men brought their censers before God and were standing in front of the tabernacle, and they gathered the entire congregation against Moses and Aaron.

> *And Moses said: "By this you shall know that the LORD has sent me to do all these works, for I have not done them of my own will. If these men die naturally like all men, or if they are visited by the common fate of all men, then the LORD has not sent me. But if the LORD creates a new thing, and the earth opens its mouth and swallows them up with all that belongs to them, and they go down alive into the pit, then you will understand that these men have rejected the LORD." Now it came to pass, as he finished speaking all these words, that the ground split apart under them, and the earth opened its mouth and swallowed them up, with their households and all the men with Korah, with all their goods. So they and all those with them went down alive into the pit; the earth closed over them, and they perished from among the assembly. Then all Israel who were around them fled at their cry, for they said, "Lest the earth swallow us up also!" And a fire came out from the LORD and consumed the two hundred and fifty men who were offering incense. (Num 16:28-35 NKJV)*

Now one would think that the congregation would have learnt a lesson from this, but look what happened the very next day:

> *On the next day all the congregation of the children of Israel complained against Moses and Aaron, saying, "You have killed the people of the LORD." Now it happened, when the congregation had gathered against Moses and Aaron, that they turned toward the tabernacle of meeting; and suddenly the cloud covered it, and the glory of the LORD appeared. Then Moses and Aaron came before the tabernacle of meeting. And the LORD spoke to Moses, saying, "Get away from among this congregation, that I may consume them in a moment." And they fell on their faces. So Moses said to Aaron, "Take a censer and put fire in it from the altar, put incense on it, and take it quickly to the congregation and make atonement*

> *for them; for wrath has gone out from the LORD. The plague has begun." Then Aaron took it as Moses commanded, and ran into the midst of the assembly; and already the plague had begun among the people. So he put in the incense and made atonement for the people. And he stood between the dead and the living; so the plague was stopped. Now those who died in the plague were fourteen thousand seven hundred, besides those who died in the Korah incident. So Aaron returned to Moses at the door of the tabernacle of meeting, for the plague had stopped. (Num 16:41-50 NKJV)*

Here is another example:

> *Now Israel remained in Acacia Grove, and the people began to commit harlotry with the women of Moab. They invited the people to the sacrifices of their gods, and the people ate and bowed down to their gods. So Israel was joined to Baal of Peor, and the anger of the LORD was aroused against Israel. Then the LORD said to Moses, "Take all the leaders of the people and hang the offenders before the LORD, out in the sun, that the fierce anger of the LORD may turn away from Israel." So Moses said to the judges of Israel, "Every one of you kill his men who were joined to Baal of Peor." And indeed, one of the children of Israel came and presented to his brethren a Midianite woman in the sight of Moses and in the sight of all the congregation of the children of Israel, who were weeping at the door of the tabernacle of meeting. Now when Phinehas the son of Eleazar, the son of Aaron the priest, saw it, he rose from among the congregation and took a javelin in his hand; and he went after the man of Israel into the tent and thrust both of them through, the man of Israel, and the woman through her body. So the plague was stopped among the children of Israel. And those who died in the plague were twenty-four thousand. (Num 25:1-9 NKJV)*

Later we read about Israel being exiled to Babylon by king Nebuchadnezzar and being stricken by all sorts of calamities due to their inability to live up to the standards of the law, thereby bringing into fulfillment the promise that they would be captured and taken to another country in Deuteronomy 28:36 (above).

Still Living According to the Law?

Now after just reading how people were treated under that Old Covenant, the saddest part is that the majority of the church today still tries to live according to the Old Covenant Law and then they wonder why they are sick, poor, depressed, unhappy and dying? The reality is that Jesus died on the cross to carry the curses of the law for us:

> *Christ has redeemed us from the curse of the law, having become a curse for us (for it is written, "Cursed is everyone who hangs on a tree") that the blessing of Abraham might come upon the Gentiles in Christ Jesus, that we might receive the promise of the Spirit through faith. (Gal 3:13-14 NKJV)*

The following are examples of how the law can creep up on the church today:

- Sitting in a "Christian" meeting where the 10 Commandments or some of the other laws in the Bible are read and we are told this is what we have to do to be blessed or accepted by God.

- Feeling guilty or condemned that we don't do enough for God or that we don't go to church, pray or read the Bible enough.

- Feeling that God doesn't hear our prayers because we have sinned in some way.

- Lacking boldness to approach God with confidence when we pray because we think He may be angry at us for something we've done.

- Trying in our own efforts to be a "better person" or be "more holy" so that God can be pleased with us.

All of the above symptoms are signs that the law is trying to creep up on us. The Bible says there is now no more law and where there is no law, there is no transgression of that law.

> *…because the law brings about wrath; for where there is no law there is no transgression. (Rom 4:15 NKJV)*

Remember how Israel's failure to comply with the law brought about the wrath of God? That's exactly what this verse is talking about, namely that the law brought about God's wrath.

No Law… Again

At the beginning of this chapter we talked about how God didn't punish people for their transgressions, from Adam up to when He gave Israel the law, because during that period there was nothing to measure their level of obedience against. Just like it was back then, so there is now no law for God to measure our performance against. He can therefore not punish us or count our sins against us anymore, because the law was crucified with Jesus!

> *...having wiped out the handwriting of requirements that was against us, which was contrary to us. And He has taken it out of the way, having nailed it to the cross. (Col 2:14 NKJV)*

No human being has ever been able to live up to the requirements of the law and no one ever will. God knew this and therefore He sent His Son Jesus in the form of a human to accomplish this feat on our behalf:

> *For what the law could not do in that it was weak through the flesh, God did by sending His own Son in the likeness of sinful flesh, on account of sin: He condemned sin in the flesh, that the righteous requirement of the law might be fulfilled in us who do not walk according to the flesh but according to the Spirit. But you are not in the flesh but in the Spirit, if indeed the Spirit of God dwells in you. Now if anyone does not have the Spirit of Christ, he is not His. (Rom 8:3-4, 9 NKJV)*

These first two verses say that the righteous requirements of the law (in other words 100% obedience ALL of the time) were met by Jesus. And Jesus then also took upon Himself the full punishment for the sin of the entire world (because according to the law, sin *had* to be punished) even though He didn't deserve it. Thereby the punishment of sin was served once and for all! Jesus justified all of those who put their faith in Him, bringing peace between God and mankind once again:

> *Therefore, having been justified by faith, we have peace with God through our Lord Jesus Christ. (Rom 5:1 NKJV)*

The following verse clenches it:

> *For until the law sin was in the world, but sin is not imputed when there is no law. (Rom 5:13 NKJV)*

This verse says that before the law had been given, even though people sinned, God didn't count their sins against them because in essence there was no law to break. And now since there is now no more law to keep or to break either, we can approach God with boldness, even if we have just messed up! Because where there is no law there is no transgression of the law. And where there is no transgression, there is no punishment.

Law →✝→ Grace

The Parable of the Prodigal Son (Luke 15)

Two alternative names for this parable could have been "**The Parable of the Angry Elder Brother**" (the attitude of much of the church today) or "**The Parable of the Loving Father**".

Note that the son was a "SON" first before he became the "prodigal son". This implies that Jesus was not talking about an unbeliever that receives salvation for the first time, but about a born again believer that went out from his father's house to live according to the desires of his flesh. Then when the son beat himself up and groveled in self pity and guilt about how unworthy he was, thinking his father was going to punish or reject him because of the sins he had committed (does this sound familiar?), note that his Father did not love him any more or any less. In fact when he returned home his Father didn't even want to listen to his confession, but simply overwhelmed him with kisses and affection flowing from His heart of love.

We sometimes forget that God has already forgiven all our sins (past present and future):

> ...that is, that God was in Christ reconciling the world to Himself, not imputing their trespasses to them... (2 Cor 5:19a NKJV)

He is always on the edge of ambushing us with another wave of His goodness. It is not our confession of mistakes that "restores" God's approval of us – we were already reconciled with Him over 2000 years ago when Jesus took our punishment on Himself and He has been pleased with us ever since. By putting our faith in God's grace, we become partakers of all the benefits of the New Covenant including a new born again nature, having the person of the Holy Spirit living inside us, as well as healing, deliverance, blessings, life, wealth and much, much more!

This parable also illustrates that born again believers can live subject to the laws of this world if they live in unbelief of God's promises. It is actually possible to live like a pauper in the house of a King! Yes God has given us precious promises in His Word, but we have to believe in them to receive them. Bad choices and our refusal to believe in God's goodness and His attitude of favor towards us may have dire consequences for us in our lives here on earth:

> *For he who sows to his flesh will of the flesh reap corruption, but he who sows to the Spirit will of the Spirit reap everlasting life. (Gal 6:8 NKJV)*

This corruption refers to suffering loss in the natural realm. If we sow to the flesh we will *not* have our minds renewed, *not* walk in the promises of God (because we will persist in unbelief) and *not* live life to its fullest in our Father's house.

> *Now I say that the heir, as long as he is a child, does not differ at all from a slave, though he is master of all, but is under guardians and stewards until the time appointed by the father. <u>Even so we, when we were children, were in bondage under the elements of the world.</u> But when the fullness of the time had come, God sent forth His Son, born of a woman, born under the law, to redeem those who were under the law, that we might receive the adoption as sons. And because you are sons, God has sent forth the Spirit of His Son into your hearts, crying out, "Abba, Father!" Therefore you are no longer a slave but a son, and if a son, then an heir of God through Christ. But then, indeed, when you did not know God, you served those which by nature are not gods. <u>But now after you have known God, or rather are known by God, how is it that you turn again to the weak and beggarly elements, to which you desire again to be in bondage?</u> You observe days and months and seasons and years. (Gal 4:1-10 NKJV, emphasis added)*

When believers begin to see that they have been *truly* set free from the law (including observing the Sabbath and all the other commandments), it will not only stop them living like beggars in bondage to the elements of this world, but also bring about a divine sense of royalty - not an arrogant and prideful "I am better than others" attitude - but an inner realization of their true identity: "I am a citizen of heaven and my Father is the King of the universe."

However, even if we do stumble into what the world sees as some *huge* sin (the prodigal son spent half of *all* the money his father had on sleeping with prostitutes and consumed everything on his fleshly lusts) there is still grace upon grace for us from God.

> *But where sin abounded, grace abounded much more. (Rom 5:20b NKJV)*

"Older Brother Syndrome"

Like the older brother, fellow believers may choose to judge a backslidden Christian for the things he / she has done, but God will never judge His children nor be angry with them ever again according to the covenant He made:

> *For this is like the waters of Noah to Me; For as I have sworn that the waters of Noah would no longer cover the earth, so have I sworn that I would not be angry with you, nor rebuke you. For the mountains shall depart and the hills be removed, but My kindness shall not depart from you, nor shall My covenant of peace be removed," says the LORD, who has mercy on you. (Isa 54:9-10 NKJV)*

Just like many Christians today, the older brother, when he saw his Father showering love on a person that didn't deserve it, became angry and resentful. This is what being under the law does to a person. The legalists work and work their backsides off for God and think that He owes it to them to bless, love and approve them in return. Look at the elder brother's words:

> *Lo, these many years I have been serving you; I never transgressed your commandment at any time. (Luke 15:29 NKJV)*

Just like many people today grade their relationship with God by how well they manage to obey the law, the older brother thought He could earn His Father's approval through his own level of obedience. And then when God blesses someone that didn't deserve it ("grace" is giving someone what they don't deserve), the legalists become angry and jealous and hate that person. Instead they should realize that none of us deserve any of it anyway and just get over it and get happy!

> *Now his older son was in the field. And as he came and drew near to the house, he heard music and dancing. (Luke 15:25 NKJV)*

Right now, this is what's happening in heaven. There is music and dancing in our Father's house! It should actually make us wonder how so many churches can be so dull, introspective, reserved, conservative and religious on Sunday mornings...

Let us therefore praise God for His grace and bask in His presence daily so that our minds will be renewed and we can start doing the works that Jesus did. And most important of all: Don't forget there's a party going on in heaven! God is pleased with us in spite of our mistakes. He is happy! He is secure in His love for us! He is in a good mood!

Law →✝→ Grace

Can a Christian "Fall Out of Grace"?

Being constantly surrounded with people and circumstances that demand from us our best performance, we can easily fall into the trap of feeling that God disapproves of us when we are not performing at our best. In our journey towards maturity in Christ however, it's quite normal for believers to make mistakes. God knew that we would not be instantly transformed in our minds when we became His children; the process of renewing our minds and overcoming old habits can sometimes take years. And in a world where churches predominantly preach law based and performance oriented living, we can often underestimate the vastness of the grace of our Father.

Let's consider whether a believer can fall "out" of the grace of God. Some people may feel that there is a sin that God can't ever forgive them for, perhaps unforgiveness towards another or maybe they've even committed adultery or murder. Let's see what the Word says.

> You have become estranged from Christ, you who attempt to be justified by law; you have fallen from grace. (Gal 5:4 NKJV)

The only way to fall out of grace is by trying to observe the law. We do *not* fall from grace when we stumble. In fact the more someone has sinned, the more grace God gives to cover that sin:

> Moreover the law entered that the offense might abound. _But where sin abounded, grace abounded much more_. (Rom 5:20 NKJV, emphasis added)

Thus, when we sin we fall *into* grace.

Sin in the Congregation

A number of Christians, when they realize this truth, go out and sin quite profusely, trying to make up for all the times they had restrained themselves previously, when they still thought that God would not accept or forgive them if they committed this or that sin. The Bible teaches us however not to indulge in the flesh:

> *For you, brethren, have been called to liberty; only do not use liberty as an opportunity for the flesh, but through love serve one another. (Gal 5:13 NKJV)*

Probably the most difficult thing for pastors / shepherds during this period is not to become anxious or insecure about their flock, even as they see how some Christians purposely set out to indulge in sin. The law preachers would say that they have now given their flock "a license to sin". This is why some preachers simply avoid teaching on grace, because they fear it would cause the church to break out into immorality. Well consider this fact: Christians sin, whether they are under law or under grace! The only difference is that grace sheds light on the sin. The problem was always there, but previously it was under the covers and grace has now brought it into the open. When someone turns on a torch in an old attic, they don't say "Look at all the dust this light has created!" No the dust was always there, the light simply exposed it.

But when a church has been established on the foundation of grace, even if some have initially set out to sin (all they will learn in any case is that sin brings about destruction, unfulfilment and bad consequences), they will always make the return to their Father when they know He loves them unconditionally, like the father loved the prodigal son in Luke 15. In fact, God's children would return faster and serve God even more than before when they realize that their destructive behavior does them no good and that only by running back to the arms of their Father will they find fulfillment in life.

Are we willing to preach grace to the extent of being misunderstood, persecuted and hated, like the apostle Paul?

> *... the ministry which I received from the Lord Jesus,* [is] *to testify to the gospel of the grace of God. (Acts 20:24b NKJV, annotations added)*

Paul was serious to the point of cursing people about this specific gospel, namely the gospel of grace!

But even if we or an angel from Heaven should preach a gospel other than the one we preached to you, let him be eternally condemned! (Gal 1:8 NKJV)

Are we willing to believe in the goodness of our Father so unconditionally that no matter where we may have run off to or what we have squandered our inheritance on, that we can still run back to our Father's house and believe we will be welcomed with open arms and a fatted calf? Yes we can believe it, God is that good!

Law →✝→ Grace

Do Christians Need to Repent?

The answer is a resounding "YES"! However the word "repent" means something entirely different than what Christians have made of it today. Bill Johnson from Bethel Church[1] in Redding, California, has often explained repentance in his own view as follows: *Re* means "again" or to "go back to". *Pent* means the top (like a penthouse). Thus combined this means to "go back to the top". This implies that when we make a mistake, all we simply have to do is change our thoughts and go back to God's thoughts towards us. And what are God's thoughts? Unconditional love and acceptance because Jesus paid the full price on our behalf.

Let's journey together and endeavor to defuse the bomb that has been crafted from this word by the modern church.

The actual Greek word for repentance, Μετάνοια (*met-an'-oy-ah*), denotes a simple change of mind that brings about a change of outward behavior. It does not however imply that we need to constantly remind ourselves of our mistakes and try to stop doing this or that deed. Doing this would only turn it into a sin management program, which is exactly what many Christians have turned their entire lives into. No, good conduct is the result of having been changed from the inside out and not something that we do in order to try to be changed.

Repentance has different implications for believers than for non believers. Basically it comes down to this: When a Christian is told to repent, it means to change their thinking about their position in Christ, or change their theology to line up with the truths of having been eternally forgiven, justified, made righteous, etc. Whenever a non believer is told to repent, it means they need to change their thinking about what Jesus means to them and come to a place where they admit they need Him as their Lord and Savior.

Let's take a look at a few examples of where the word "repent" or "repentance" was used in the New Testament. The Bible is God's love letter to His children.

Let's take the sting out of "repentance" today and see it for the beautiful thing it actually is.

Example 1

Before the cross, Jesus and John the Baptist told people to repent and to be baptized, but they were both preaching under the Old Covenant to people that were still under the law (remember the New Covenant only began after the cross). John's baptism was a baptism of repentance, pointing *non-believers* to Jesus:

> *Then Paul said, "John indeed baptized with a baptism of repentance, saying to the people that they should believe on Him who would come after him, that is, on Christ Jesus". (Acts 19:4 NKJV)*

Example 2

> *For even if I made you sorry with my letter, I do not regret it; though I did regret it. For I perceive that the same epistle made you sorry, though only for a while. Now I rejoice, not that you were made sorry, but that your sorrow led to <u>repentance</u>. For you were made sorry in a godly manner, that you might suffer loss from us in nothing. For godly sorrow produces <u>repentance</u> leading to salvation, not to be regretted; but the sorrow of the world produces death. (2 Cor 7:8-10 NKJV, emphasis added)*

Paul was writing his second epistle to the *church* in Corinth (which means they were Christians) and after his severe rebuke to them in his first letter, he was exceedingly glad they had taken his words to heart, turning away from the wicked ways in which they had previously been conducting themselves. In his previous letter he reprimanded them for practicing such wickedness as were not even known among non believers:

> *It is actually reported that there is sexual immorality among you, and such sexual immorality as is not even named among the Gentiles – that a man has his father's wife! (1 Cor 5:1 NKJV)*

Let's look at the Greek word used for "salvation" in 2 Corinthians 7:10:

G4991 σωτηρία (so-tay-ree'-ah)

> Feminine of a derivative of G4990 as (properly abstract) noun; rescue or safety (physically or morally): - deliver, health, salvation, save, saving.

Paul wasn't saying that these believers were going to lose their salvation if they persisted with these evil works; he was saying that their turning away from these things actually saved them from a whole heap of heartache, pain and dire consequences later on. Just imagine the conflict that would exist in a church if it became known that a boy was sleeping with his mother!

But because these people changed their thinking and realized that their conduct was actually not in line with their identity as purified, cleansed and forgiven believers, they were motivated to change their ways, hence Paul's praise for them in this, his second letter:

> *Great is my boldness of speech toward you, great is my boasting on your behalf. I am filled with comfort. I am exceedingly joyful in all our tribulation. (2 Cor 7:4 NKJV)*

It's worth noting that their motivation to change their behavior was neither a threat of punishment nor the danger of losing their salvation: it was the revelation that they were unconditionally loved by God in spite of their evil conduct! God's promises and love to them remained true in spite of their conduct and this brought about their change of heart. Look at the opening words of this same chapter:

> *Therefore, <u>having these promises</u>, beloved, let us cleanse ourselves from all filthiness of the flesh... (2 Cor 7:1a NKJV, emphasis added)*

Paul told them that *because* they had God's promises (of love, blessing, eternal life, etc.) they should get their act together, not that God was going to reject or punish them for their transgressions.

Example 3

> *Truly, these times of ignorance God overlooked, but now commands all men everywhere to <u>repent</u>. (Act 17:30 NKJV, emphasis added)*

In this chapter Paul was preaching to non-believers in Athens:

> *Now while Paul waited for them at Athens, his spirit was provoked within him when he saw that the city was given over to idols. Therefore he reasoned in the synagogue with the Jews and with the Gentile worshipers, and in the marketplace daily with those who happened to be there. (Act 17:16-17 NKJV)*

Paul was telling these people who were wholly given to idolatry, to repent and be saved. He urged them to place their trust in the "unknown" God in verse 23. They had so many gods and temples and statues in their city that someone had even erected an altar that had been dedicated to the "Unknown God". Paul then used this as an opportunity to tell them about Jesus Christ and the resurrection, whereof they had no prior knowledge. And by God's grace, some were born again that day!

Example 4

> *"Therefore, King Agrippa, I was not disobedient to the heavenly vision, but declared first to those in Damascus and in Jerusalem, and throughout all the region of Judea, and then to the Gentiles, that they should <u>repent</u>, turn to God, and do works befitting <u>repentance.</u> (Act 26:19-20 NKJV, emphasis added)*

Here Paul explained how he told the Gentiles (unbelievers) to repent (become born again) and then, just as in our example 2, he motivated them to afterwards do works that corresponded with who they would become after they had repented: Sanctified, forgiven, holy born again believers. These two verses therefore pertain to non believers and then also to believers.

Example 5

> *...how I kept back nothing that was helpful, but proclaimed it to you, and taught you publicly and from house to house, testifying to Jews, and also to Greeks, <u>repentance</u> toward God and faith toward our Lord Jesus Christ. (Act 20:20-21 NKJV, emphasis added)*

Again Paul was telling non-believers to put their faith in Christ (as in example 2), calling it "repentance toward God".

Repentance From Dead Works

Probably one of the most important verses concerning repentance is found in Hebrews 6. This book was written to Jews who had become born again, but they were still holding on to some of their traditions and law abiding customs. They were however Christians.

> *Therefore, leaving the discussion of the elementary principles of Christ, let us go on to perfection, not laying again the foundation of <u>repentance from dead works</u> and of faith toward God. (Heb 6:1 NKJV, emphasis added)*

The writer of Hebrews was listing a few basic foundations of the Christian faith, amongst others "repentance from dead works". When we try to earn God's approval by reading more Bible, tithing, praying long prayers, joining outreach ministries or even giving all that we have away, it is called "dead works", because our security and feeling of belonging is based on what we do and not on what Jesus has done for us.

In broad terms the book of Hebrews is a summary of the superiority of the New Covenant over the Old, with the New Covenant based on the finished work of the cross and us simply believing in what God has already done for us and the Old Covenant based on ceremonious law keeping and religion, based on inferior promises and the traditions of men. Therefore in Hebrews 6:1 above, the writer was not talking about us having to repent of our sins, but instead to stop trying to earn our salvation and to stop trying so hard to please God, because He is already pleased with us since we are His children!

To summarize, when a non believer repents it means they put their faith in God and become born again. When a believer repents it simply means they change their thinking to line up with God's thoughts, turning away from deeds that do not portray their true identity as a forgiven, purified believer. It also means turning away from dead works, which means to quit trying to be justified through their own level of obedience and beginning to rely on the finished work of the cross and the blood of Jesus, which grants believers unrestricted access to God's favor and acceptance.

To repent does not mean to sit in sackcloth and ash and plead with God for forgiveness every time we make a mistake, as this would be disregarding the once for all, 100% perfect sacrifice of Christ and believing that our sin is more powerful than the blood of Christ:

> *By that will we have been sanctified through the offering of the body of Jesus Christ <u>once for all</u>. (Heb 10:10 NKJV, emphasis added)*

Law →✝→ Grace

Approaching God with Boldness

After clothing us with His own spotless garment of righteousness, God does not want us to be conscious of our sins anymore, like the people were under the Old Covenant. Trying to live according to the requirements of the law will make us all too aware of just how poorly we measure up against it. The only way for a believer to have confidence when approaching God is to be absolutely convinced that all their sins have been forgiven! Anything less will always leave a trace of uncertainty about whether God really loves them or wants to bless them. God wants us to be conscious of our righteousness. When we constantly tell God how sorry we are for this and that sin, we remind ourselves of how bad *we think* we are, forgetting that our sin was already forgiven at the cross more than 2000 years ago!

The writer of Hebrews wanted to instill in his readers this same confidence, showing them how the superiority of the New Covenant over the Old allows the believer to draw near to God with boldness, trusting not in their own level of obedience to the law, but in the blood of Christ. Those who try to please God through their own efforts of law keeping are like the priests of the Old Covenant who constantly remained conscious of their mistakes, because no human being was or is ever able to perfectly execute the obligations of the law:

> For the law, having a shadow of the good things to come, and not the very image of the things, can never with these same sacrifices, which they offer continually year by year, make those who approach perfect. For then would they not have ceased to be offered? For the worshipers, once purified, would have had no more consciousness of sins. But in those sacrifices there is a reminder of sins every year. For it is not possible that the blood of bulls and goats could take away sins. (Heb 10:1-4, NKJV)

> But this Man [Jesus], after He had offered one sacrifice for sins for ever, sat down at the right hand of God, from that time waiting

> *till His enemies are made His footstool. For by one offering He has perfected for ever those who are being sanctified. (Heb 10:12-14 NKJV)*

> *Therefore, brethren, having boldness to enter the Holiest by the blood of Jesus, by a new and living way which He consecrated for us, through the veil, that is, His flesh, and having a High Priest over the house of God, let us draw near with a true heart in full assurance of faith, having our hearts sprinkled from an evil conscience and our bodies washed with pure water. Let us hold fast the confession of our hope without wavering, for He who promised is faithful. (Heb 10:19-23 NKJV)*

Being Aware of Who We ARE

Which of the following attitudes would Christ rather want us to walk around with: Feeling condemned, unworthy and guilty, begging and crawling on our knees before Him, constantly pleading for mercy? While at the same time having no confidence whatsoever to approach Him because we feel we are sinners? Or would God rather want us to be conscious of the fact that we have been completely forgiven of all sins (past present and future), fully accepted and loved by Him, how we have been justified and made righteous and given authority over sickness, poverty and all other enemies of God?

We have even been seated in heavenly places with Christ!

> *...and raised us up together, and made us sit together in the heavenly places in Christ Jesus. (Eph 2:6 NKJV)*

Now how can a believer who sits in heaven still think that they are a sinner? This can only happen when we try to relate to God on the basis of how well we have performed, forgetting that this is *not the way that He relates to us.* God is a Spirit and He relates Spirit to Spirit. And since the Spirit of a believer has been sanctified, perfected, purified and justified, this is the way that God sees us.

In Matthew 3 we see Jesus being baptized in the river Jordan. This was before He had done any miracles, before He began His ministry and before He had healed even a single person. After He was baptized the heavens opened, the Holy Spirit came down onto Him like a dove and the Father said "This is My beloved Son in whom I am well pleased." What makes this so remarkable is the fact that Jesus was accepted and loved by God *before* He even did one miracle or began His ministry. Why then did God love Him already? Because Jesus was God's Son - simple as that. By the way it isn't written anywhere that the heavens ever closed again or that the Holy Spirit ever "lifted" off Him again.

Now the Bible tells us over and over that because of our faith in Christ, we are God's children too.

> *The Spirit Himself bears witness with our spirit that we are children of God. (Rom 8:16 NKJV)*

In fact we are even called God's SONS, just like Jesus:

> *"I will be a Father to you, and you shall be My sons and daughters, says the LORD Almighty". (2 Cor 6:18 NKJV)*

Now if God loved Jesus at that stage, regardless of the fact that He hadn't done any miracles, didn't have a ministry or hadn't even preached a sermon yet, wouldn't God, because He is the same for ever, love us in the same way?

We can therefore, whether we feel like He loves us or not, whether we think we've committed the worst sin or whether we feel like we've been wasting our lives with insignificant activities, trust that God rejoices over us simply because of our identity: We are His beloved children, bought with the most precious commodity in the universe: The blood of Christ:

> *...knowing that you were not redeemed with corruptible things, like silver or gold, from your aimless conduct received by tradition from your fathers, but with the precious blood of Christ, as of a lamb without blemish and without spot. (1 Pet 1:18-19 NKJV)*

God is pleased with us, whether we do miracles or have a ministry, OR NOT.

Law →✝→ Grace

What is the Unforgivable Sin?

This issue hangs over the heads of millions of Christians like a heavy fog that just simply will not clear away. Mostly this question is asked by those who do not yet have a full revelation of the Father's true nature. Jesus accurately portrayed the Father's nature (having had firsthand experience in heaven) when He told the parable of the prodigal son. Even though believers agree that we are saved through faith, there still remains with some people a slight "caution" of God, a fear of rejection or punishment for not continually performing at our best, or perhaps failing to confess some hidden or forgotten sin.

The following verse is commonly quoted:

> *...but he who blasphemes against the Holy Spirit never has forgiveness, but is subject to eternal condemnation. (Mark 3:29 NKJV)*

Blaspheming against the Holy Spirit indirectly implies that such a person has not yet been saved. Here's why: The moment someone is born again they are filled and sealed with the Holy Spirit:

> *In Him you also trusted, after you heard the word of truth, the gospel of your salvation; in whom also, having believed, you were sealed with the Holy Spirit of promise. (Eph 1:13 NKJV)*

The Holy Spirit cannot blaspheme against Himself, because since He is God this would mean He is blaspheming against God. No, the Holy Spirit glorifies the Father and testifies to the fact that Jesus had come in the flesh:

> *By this you know the Spirit of God: Every spirit that confesses that Jesus Christ has come in the flesh is of God. (1 John 4:2 NKJV)*

So this means that no person that has been given the Holy Spirit, can *speaking by the spirit* blaspheme against God. If a person blasphemes against the Holy Spirit, it means the Spirit they have is not the Holy Spirit, which means *they have not yet been saved* and therefore cannot be forgiven for their sin (because they don't believe in Jesus). However once such a person repents and puts their faith in Christ, *all* their sins are forgiven.

When we sin, we fall *into* grace. The bigger our sin, the bigger the grace that covers the sin, according to Romans 5:20 (and remember we're not encouraging people to go out and sin). If we ever think that there's a sin that cannot be covered by God's grace, we are actually saying that the punishment that was bestowed on Jesus was not harsh enough and that our sin is more powerful than the power of His forgiveness! Those who do this are trampling the grace of God under foot.

Only One Unforgivable Sin

There is one sin however, that can't be forgiven. And this is also a very misunderstood scripture...

Jesus had just told His disciples He would be going away, but that He would send the Helper to them; the promised Holy Spirit:

> *And when He* [the Holy Spirit] *has come, He will convict the world of sin, and of righteousness, and of judgment: (John 16:8 NKJV, annotations added)*

Most people stop here and think this verse means the Holy Spirit's job is to convict them of sin; that He is always supposed to make them feel guilty about "unholy areas" in their life. However most people miss the fact that there is a semi colon at the end of verse 8. This means that Jesus was about to explain what He had just said! So let's read the next verses as well:

> *⁸ And when He has come, He will convict the world of sin, and of righteousness, and of judgment: ⁹ of sin, because they do not believe in Me; ¹⁰ of righteousness, because I go to My Father and you see Me no more; ¹¹ of judgment, because the ruler of this world is judged. (John 16:8-10 NKJV)*

Verse 9 says the Holy Spirit will convict the world of their *sin of unbelief in Jesus*, thus He is referring to unbelievers. Also, it says "sin", not "sins". Unbelief in Jesus Christ is the *only sin* that Jesus could not die for. This is the only sin that God can't forgive. A person has to believe in Jesus if they want to be saved!

The above verses also say that the Holy Spirit will convict people of two other things:

Verse 10 – of righteousness, because Jesus went to the Father, and imputed His righteousness to believers as a free gift!

Verse 11 – of judgment, because Satan (the ruler of this world) is judged!

So the Holy Spirit really only reminds us of how righteous we are in Christ, how powerless Satan is, and He reminds unbelievers that they need to believe in Jesus. What an awesome God we serve!

So if we still live with some secret fear of punishment, then we have not yet received the full revelation of the grace and love of our Father:

> *There is no fear in love; but perfect love casts out fear, because fear involves torment* [punishment]. *But he who fears has not been made perfect in love. (1 John 4:18 NKJV, annotations added)*

Knowing how much our Father loves us will cast out all fear of punishment, because we have been made righteous forever!

Law →✝→ Grace

Reading the Bible in Context

Whenever the Bible is read today it has to be read in its correct context, or we can be conned by the text (con - text, get it?). The Word is life; the Word is truth; the Name of the Word is Jesus.

> *In the beginning was the Word, and the Word was with God, and the Word was God. (John 1:1 NKJV)*

When people quote Bible verses out of context, it is almost as though they are writing their own version of the Bible, creating their own God! Today *seemingly* condemning verses are thrown out of context at believers of the grace message, or to keep entire church congregations "under control". Although those who do this won't admit it, they are actually operating in partnership with the devil, attempting to bring God's children under the fear and control of man (the pastor / preacher).

It's easy to spot this phenomenon in a church: Since such preachers constantly desire to be in control, they will very seldom or almost never make room for the Holy Spirit to move unhindered in their services. There will always be a set program to follow and the whole thing will be precisely orchestrated from start to finish. These leaders have their grip firmly clenched around the neck of the church, but a time is approaching where God will say to these modern day Pharaohs: "Let my people go!"

Bible verses are also used out of context to formulate excuses and doctrines for our lack of power and to legitimize the absence of signs and wonders in our lives and ministries. The truth is that we should never water the Bible down to our own level of experience, but rather live to see the supernatural realm of heaven break into our own lives!

> *Indeed, let God be true but every man a liar. (Rom 3:4 NKJV)*

Andre van der Merwe

Truth is measured by the standard of the Word of God and not by man's experience! The supernatural signs and wonders and the miracles of God were not just meant for the times of the Bible, they are for today as well – the Word is just as powerful today as it ever was!

> *Heaven and earth will pass away, but My words will by no means pass away. (Mark 13:31 NKJV)*

Getting the Covenants Right

When reading any Bible verse, we have to know under which covenant it falls. To recap (from the chapter entitled "Three Covenants"), there were largely three important periods in the Bible:

First Period: From the Garden of Eden up to Mount Sinai where the law was given. During this period which lasted several thousand years, people were not under the law and God bestowed unconditional love and kindness on them apart from their works.

Second Period: From Mount Sinai up to the cross. Just because certain Bible books fall after the blank page that the Bible Society put in our Bible, it doesn't necessarily mean they are in the New Covenant. When reading the four gospels as well as certain scriptures further in the New Testament, it has to be established if the text refers to the Old Covenant Law or to New Covenant grace. Jesus spoke predominantly about the kingdom of heaven, but most of the time He spoke to crowds of people that were still under the mindset of the Old Covenant Law that God had given to Moses and Israel. Jesus had to counter their religious thinking, sometimes using very harsh words. On the contrary we mostly see Him extending compassion and grace whenever He addressed sinners who humbled themselves.

Third Period: From the cross onwards, what we know as the New Covenant. In the New Covenant God does not deal with us as believers based on our level of obedience, but on the basis of Jesus' obedience on our behalf. God loves us and blesses us regardless of our performance.

There are also further means to establish what the context of scriptures are, such as studying Bible history or Bible commentaries to know by whom the specific book was written, to whom it was addressed, why and when it was written, etc. Here are three examples of misquoted scriptures:

Example 1

> *And if your eye causes you to sin, pluck it out and cast it from you. It is better for you to enter into life with one eye, rather than having two eyes, to be cast into hell fire. (Matt 18:9 NKJV)*

> *But I say to you that whoever looks at a woman to lust for her has already committed adultery with her in his heart. (Matt 5:28 NKJV)*

To establish the context for these verses, let's look at which period it falls into. Jesus spoke these words before He went to the cross and in this instance He was addressing people who prided themselves in having the law and commandments that God gave to Moses and Israel. So generally we would expect His words to be as sharp as a knife.

Through the centuries these people had watered the law down to a standard that they could "keep". Here Jesus was simply telling them that the standards of the law were much higher than any man could ever hope to keep and that mankind really needs a Savior! In essence He was saying "The standards of the law are so high that you'd have to mutilate yourself if you wanted to fulfill its requirements". These verses are Old Covenant Law and not meant for believers to try and live by.

Example 2

> *Whoever commits sin also commits lawlessness, and sin is lawlessness. And you know that He was manifested to take away our sins, and in Him there is no sin. Whoever abides in Him does not sin. Whoever sins has neither seen Him nor known Him. (1 John 3:4-6 NKJV)*

These verses are almost near the end of the Bible, which means they could possibly be New Covenant. But at a first glance they seem so condemning! Whenever this happens, it's always good to read the surrounding verses and if need be, the entire book as well. Let's read the next few verses too:

> *Little children, let no one deceive you. He who practices righteousness is righteous, just as He is righteous. He who sins is of the devil, for the devil has sinned from the beginning. For this purpose the Son of God was manifested, that He might destroy the works of the devil. <u>Whoever has been born of God does not sin,</u> for His seed remains in him; <u>and he cannot sin,</u> because he has been born of God. (1 John 3:7-9 NKJV, emphasis added)*

The apostle John was writing to his "little children" to encourage them and establish them in the revelation of just how secure they were in Christ. They had just come out from under the influence of teachers of Gnosticism and John was by no means trying to scare his beloved flock or point out their mistakes. Instead he was speaking about their sheltered position in Christ. The key is the first part of verse 9: *"Whoever has been born of God does not sin"*.

But how can this be? Since we *all* make mistakes sometimes, does this mean that *nobody* is born of God? The reason why John can make such a statement is evident: Any person that has been born of God is made a partaker of the nature of God; such a person derives their life and very inner character from God.

> *But he who is joined to the Lord is one spirit with Him. (1 Cor 6:17 NKJV)*

This principle of divine life (called the Seed of God) remains spotless and untainted in that person regardless of their behavior, because it is impossible to corrupt the nature of God. So it is clear that the context of this book is not about man's *behavior*, but about their *position*. In a later chapter we will discuss the issue of whether a believer still has a sinful nature.

A born again believer is the righteousness of God and whether we do good or bad, we remain righteous. That's how Abraham stayed righteous even though he lied to Pharaoh about his wife. That doesn't make lying or sinning right, but it explains how we stay the righteousness of God even when we make mistakes.

Example 3

> *Do not be deceived, God is not mocked; for whatever a man sows, that he will also reap. For he who sows to his flesh will of the flesh reap corruption, but he who sows to the Spirit will of the Spirit reap everlasting life. (Gal 6:7-8 NKJV)*

It seems as though these verse are saying that God will ensure that every person who commits a transgression will receive their just reward for it, namely punishment. This doesn't seem to fit the context of the New Covenant and the picture of a God of love, grace and kindness. Secondly it also seems contrary to the fact that Jesus had already been punished for the sin of the entire world. It seems to contradict the principles of the New Covenant, saying that we will get good if we do good, but that we will get bad if we do bad (which of course is exactly what the Old Covenant Law says). Lastly it also doesn't seem to fit the context of the book of Galatians - one of Paul's masterpieces on justification through faith apart from the works of the law; that a person is declared righteous on the basis of their belief in Jesus and not through their level of obedience. Therefore we need to read the other verses around this verse to get a better understanding of what it is saying. Let's go back as far as the end of the previous chapter:

> *I say then: Walk in the Spirit, and you shall not fulfill the lust of the flesh. For the flesh lusts against the Spirit, and the Spirit against the flesh; and these are contrary to one another, so that you do not do the things that you wish. But if you are led by the Spirit, you are not under the law. Now the works of the flesh are evident, which are: adultery, fornication, uncleanness, lewdness, idolatry, sorcery, hatred, contentions, jealousies, outbursts of wrath, selfish ambitions, dissensions, heresies, envy, murders, drunkenness, revelries, and the like; of which I tell you beforehand, just as I also told you in time past, that those who practice such things will not inherit the kingdom of God. But the fruit of the Spirit is love, joy, peace, longsuffering, kindness, goodness, faithfulness, gentleness, self-control. Against such there is no law. (Gal 5:16-23 NKJV)*
>
> *<u>Do not be deceived, God is not mocked; for whatever a man sows, that he will also reap.</u> For he who <u>sows to his flesh will of the flesh reap corruption,</u> but he who sows to the Spirit will of the Spirit reap everlasting life. And let us not grow weary <u>while doing good,</u> for in due season we shall reap if we do not lose heart. Therefore, as we have opportunity, let us <u>do good to all,</u> especially to those who are of the household of faith. (Gal 6:7-10 NKJV, emphasis added)*

When we as New Covenant believers sow to the flesh (which means to follow after the desires of the unrenewed part of our mind) and according to Galatians 5:19-21 we indulge in the "works of the flesh" (which includes envy, murders, fornication, etc), we are certain to run into trouble with other people or even at some point with the laws of the local government or country that we live in. Our wrong actions have consequences in the earth, which is what the "corruption" refers to in Galatians 6:8a:

> *For he who sows to his flesh will of the <u>flesh</u> reap corruption... (Gal 6:8a NKJV, emphasis added)*

Note that it says "...will of the *<u>flesh</u>* reap corruption..." which refers to natural, earthly consequences.

All the eternal judgment and punishment was carried by Jesus on our behalf, and therefore the corruption is not referring to a spiritual corruption. The Seed of God living on the inside of a believer can never be corrupted!

> *...having been born again, not of corruptible seed but incorruptible, through the word of God which lives and abides for ever. (1 Pet 1:23 NKJV)*

So whenever we encounter verses in the Bible that seem "scary" or condemning, we need to put on our "grace lenses" so we can read these verses through the filter of the blood of Jesus by which we have been forgiven and perfected:

> *For by one offering he hath perfected for ever them that are sanctified. (Heb 10:14 KJV)*

We can never reduce the Bible to our level of experience, but we should rather contend for our experience to be raised up to the level of the everlasting Word.

Law →✝→ Grace

Powerless Religion

There is a growing frustration and an increased awareness in the earth that there is something wrong with the "average" way church is being done today. Millions of people have found that simply going through the motions of getting up for work every week day, taking it easy on Saturdays and finally going to the local church for a little Sunday "fix-up" has not been very fulfilling. In contrast, the church in Acts saw dead people raised, all sorts of diseases healed, literally had their buildings shaken by the power of God (Acts 4:31) and got together *daily* to have fellowship with each other (Acts 2:46).

The main cause for the sorry state that much of today's church finds itself in, is the destructive force called "religion". Religion found its way into the New Covenant Church almost immediately after the church's inception. This was mainly due to the traditions which had been propagated for centuries mainly by the Jews, but also by the Gentiles worshipping their pagan gods. After Peter's first sermon where 3000 got saved, the church immediately begun moving in mighty signs and wonders, fulfilling the great commission of taking the gospel to the nations of the world and living in freedom, grace and love. They saw mighty miracles happen in their midst and had a burning passion for God.

Then came religion with its rules, regulations and traditions and swept the earth as we know it into almost 1500 years of what was known as the "dark ages". Apart from a few exceptions, development in technology, arts, literature and science slowed down significantly, because religion doesn't limit itself just to the church – it influences all of society and engrains itself into all aspects of humanity.

During this period the church battled for control of the biggest part of the known world and through sheer terror forced their ways and beliefs onto every person, from the least to the greatest. These wars or crusades[1] as they were called, raged for a few centuries against Muslims, Jews, Orthodox Christians and others. Most secular historians claim that this era came to an end through a movement / period called the Renaissance[2], an era of cultural and educational reform that saw the development of linear perspective in painting, social and political upheaval and revolutions in many intellectual pursuits.

The Reformation

Most theologians claim however that it was the restoration of the knowledge of God's goodness that brought about the end of the "dark ages". Religion was what started it, and it was the destruction (or partial destruction) of religion that ended this sad period of human history. This movement was called the Protestant Reformation[3] and started in 1517 when the light of Romans 1:16-17 dawned on a monk named Martin Luther, who shook his fist at the religious system and challenged it.

> *For I am not ashamed of the gospel of Christ, for it is the power of God unto salvation to everyone who believes, to the Jew first and also to the Greek, For in it the righteousness of God is revealed from faith to faith; as it is written, "The just shall live by faith".* (Rom 1:16-17 NKJV)

Martin Luther had spent years trying to "purify" himself before God, spent days and days confessing his sins, tried to live as holy as he could and after doing all this he found that he could never manage to make the underlying sense of condemnation go away. Imagine the courage of this one man taking on a system that threatened to kill scientists who said the earth was round; a system of control that had forced itself onto society and ushered fear into the hearts of all those who opposed it!

The main reason that we are not seeing the mighty signs and wonders today that the church in Acts saw, is because we are still battling with the remnant of almost 1500 years of "dark ages"; of people being scared and bashed with the laws of the Bible to bring them under the fear and control of man. Even today the majority of people in church leadership have their grips locked firmly around the noose of their congregations, fearful of letting their flock explore for themselves the realms of freedom that exist in God. It is professed that people have to be controlled instead of being brought into liberty, as liberty is viewed as a license to indulge in sin.

As Rob Rufus from City Church International[4] points out: *The church today does not need another spiritual revival (because revivals come and go); it needs another theological reformation as it did in the days of Martin Luther! Reformation will automatically bring about revival.*

Remember the story about the naked king who was deceived by the spinsters who supposedly made him invisible clothes? A little child saw through their scam and shouted: "The king is naked!" In exactly the same way we need to stand up even in these days and say: "The king is naked! There is something wrong with the way the traditional church is operating! Why aren't we seeing the same miracles happening today that we saw in the Bible?"

Jesus made the following statement:

> *"Most assuredly, I say to you, he who believes in Me, the works that I do he will do also; and greater works than these he will do, because I go to My Father". (John 14:12 NKJV)*

Was Jesus lying? Was He a cruel sadist that would tell us to try and do something that He knew we would never be able to do? Of course not! Look at the last line of this verse; Jesus said we would do greater works than He did *because He would be going to the Father.* Did Jesus go to the Father? Yes. So why aren't we doing the greater works? We can't let anybody fool us into thinking that the time of miracles passed away with the early church apostles. We have the following scriptures that prove God does miracles even today:

> *Jesus Christ the same yesterday and today and for ever. (Heb 13:8 NKJV)*

> *Heaven and earth shall pass away, but My Words shall not pass away. (Mar 13:31 NKJV)*

Now if God did mighty works through the church in the times of the Bible and if God is the same for ever, then it is clear that the only thing that has changed is the church. The Bible warns us about people who try to convince the church that the time of miracles has passed away:

> *Beware lest anyone rob you through philosophy and vain deceit, according to the tradition of men, according to the elements of the world, and not according to Christ. (Col 2:8 NKJV)*

> *...making the Word of God of no effect through your tradition which you have delivered. (Mar 7:13a NKJV)*

Manmade traditions and regulations nullify the power of God's Word! They dump us into unbelief and take the romance out of our relationship with God.

We all need to have our thinking changed and our minds renewed. We need a theological reformation, a message that restores the fullness of the message of grace of the New Covenant and removes the Old Covenant Law. The law is a ministry of death (2 Corinthians 3:7) and the law is not based on faith

(Galatians 3:12): it kills faith and makes people self conscious, sin conscious and self righteous. Christians can fast and pray and sing and have conferences and all sorts of things, but if there is not a theological reformation that changes the way they think, nothing will change. We can have fools become filled with the Holy Spirit, but if they do not change their thinking, they will only be anointed fools.

A Form of Godliness vs. Real Power

Millions of Christians are happy to go to their cozy little Sunday morning meetings, listen to a sermon that makes them feel a little bit better about themselves or reminds them that they have a responsibility towards God, but that's about as far as it goes. They have a form of godliness, but don't want to hear that they have been called to walk in mighty signs and wonders; to be living administrators of the power of heaven into the earth. The Bible talks about such people:

> *...having a form of godliness but denying its power. And from such people turn away! (2 Tim 3:5 NKJV)*

The Kingdom of God is not about always having the right things to say:

> *For the kingdom of God is not in word, but in power. (1 Cor 4:20 NKJV)*

Paul also said that when the *authentic* gospel is preached it will be accompanied by signs and wonders.

> *And my speech and my preaching was not with enticing words of man's wisdom, but in demonstration of the Spirit and of power, so that your faith should not stand in the wisdom of men, but in the power of God. (1 Cor 2:4-5 NKJV)*

In fact, when the authentic Gospel of Grace is preached, God will confirm His word by signs and wonders:

> *Therefore they stayed a long time, speaking boldly in the Lord, who bore witness to the word of His grace, giving miracles and wonders to be done by their hands. (Act 14:3 NKJV, emphasis added)*

How else is the unbelieving world of today supposed to see that God really exists? Do we think that in today's modern scientific era we are going to be able to convince people with words alone? Definitely not! The current state of the world around us bears witness to this fact.

To those who are living in the captivity of dead religion, not seeing the kingdom of God manifesting in signs and wonders around them and not hearing the message of grace of the New Covenant of the Bible preached, they might want to consider that it's time to shake their fist at this destructive force and prison called "religion" and come into the freedom of Christ; the freedom that Jesus gave His life for, so that we can live free from the fear of people's opinions, free from the demands of laws and regulations and free to love God because He is a good Father!

> *Stand fast therefore in the liberty with which Christ has made us free, and do not again be held with the yoke of bondage. (Gal 5:1 NKJV)*

Law →✝→ Grace

Is Grace Simply a License to Sin?

This topic has presented itself in the form of numerous questions and statements in the past, such as the following:

- Does preaching grace lead to a careless lifestyle?

- Won't people run out and sin recklessly if they get too "deep" into the grace message?

- We cannot preach grace to new believers because they are not mature enough to be trusted with such freedom yet.

- Taking the law off believers gives them a license to sin.

All these statements fly straight in the face of what the Bible teaches about grace:

> For the grace of God that brings salvation has appeared to all men, teaching us that, denying ungodliness and worldly lusts, we should live soberly, righteously, and godly in the present age. (Tit 2:11-12 NKJV)

First let us consider how the truth of grace influences a person's thinking. When we begin to comprehend what the message of grace is all about (how God pardoned the sins of the whole world (Hebrews 10:17); abolished the written code of the law (Colossians 2:14); set people at liberty to live free from the fear of judgment and punishment (1 John 4:18); how believers are encouraged to have boldness when approaching God (Hebrews 10:19-21); that we can be confident that God will never be angry with us ever again (Isaiah 54:9-10) and many other truths like these), it is clear that a proper understanding of these matters will in fact *not* encourage a person to *want* to sin, but rather inspire such a person to be more thankful toward God for all He has done, to live a life worthy of the sacrifice made by Jesus and to deny ungodly conduct as stated in Titus 2:11-12 (above).

In Romans 4 Paul writes about this same thing:

> [5]*But to him who does not work but believes on Him who justifies the ungodly, his faith is accounted for righteousness,* [6]*just as David also describes the blessedness of the man to whom God imputes righteousness apart from works:* [7]*"Blessed are those whose lawless deeds are forgiven, and whose sins are covered;* [8]*Blessed is the man to whom the LORD shall not impute sin. (Rom 4:5-8 NKJV)*

Here Paul was quoting the words of David from Psalm 32:1-2. David was looking forward into the future and prophetically saw the New Covenant with all its benefits, such as grace, forgiveness of all sins, unconditional love and acceptance, etc. He expressed his longing to live under this covenant, since he was still bound by the law of having to perform rituals and make regular atoning sacrifices for his sins. David also wanted to live in the freedom that we now have, being justified freely through our faith in Christ.

In verse 6 we see the word "blessedness" used. The Greek form of this word is actually "blessednesses" (in the plural form). David was about to describe the *different kinds* of blessedness that believers would have under the New Covenant, hence the semicolon at the end of verse 6:

In verse 7 he said that people would firstly be blessed in the New Covenant because all their sins have been forgiven. Everything immoral they've ever done has been swept into the deepest parts of the ocean and since God is not really into deep sea diving, He's not going to go down there and dig them up again.

In verse 8 he said that people would also be blessed because God would never count any of their future mistakes against them either. Most law preachers have a major problem with this second type of blessedness, considering it to be a blank cheque to go out and sin. However the Word says what it says...

Mostly the arguments and questions against the grace message, such as the ones mentioned at the beginning of this chapter, come from people who are not necessarily afraid that they themselves will be deceived into wanting to commit more sin, but their arguments are for other "weaker" Christians who in their opinion do not yet have the maturity to handle the responsibility that comes with such freedom. Therefore they insist that the truth of the grace message be taught with a healthy dose of law mixed in to warn these "weak" Christians against the perils of sinning.

How ironic is it then that the Bible actually teaches us that sin doesn't increase through grace, but rather through the law:

> *God's law was given so that all people could see how sinful they were. But as people sinned more and more, God's wonderful grace became more abundant (Rom 5:20 NLT).*

Grace actually came in and *removed* the sin that was made more abundant through the law!

So for someone to say that grace is a license to sin, it simply serves to expose such a person's ignorance to what grace actually means and stands for. It reveals that they don't understand that the power of the Holy Spirit inside a believer (reminding them of their complete 100% righteous standing before God) is an infinitely stronger empowerment for "good behavior" than threatening someone with the law.

Therefore as a result of these truths, the legalists can all relax and come to terms with the fact that the Holy Spirit can be trusted with the transforming work in the life of a believer:

> *...being confident of this very thing, that He who has begun a good work in you will complete it until the day of Jesus Christ. (Phil 1:6 NKJV)*

Nobody appointed us as each other's moral policemen, so how can we ever try to assume that function? The truth is that grace can never be reduced to an "acceptable" level to compensate for the insecurities of legalists. Due to the extreme nature of the law, grace also needs to be preached in its purest form in order to free people from the poison and prison of "works based" mindsets.

Law →✝→ Grace

Do Christians Have a Sinful Nature? (Indwelling Sin)

Because of a regrettable misinterpretation in some translations of the Bible of the Greek word *sarx* (which directly translated means "flesh"), the doctrine of the "sinful nature" or "indwelling sin" has been propagated and preached with amazing conviction for centuries. It has caused sincere believers to try and live up to manmade moral standards, without realizing that in doing this they only subject themselves to endless frustration, lack of confidence before God and an expectation of punishment to come their way.

In the original Greek language which the New Testament was translated from, the word *sarx* was used to describe over a dozen different concepts, such as the sinful nature, human flesh, sexual intercourse, carnality, etc. The **W.E. Vines Expository Dictionary of Bible Words** lists 14 different meanings for the word *sarx*. The only way to determine the meaning of *sarx* in a particular part of scripture is to look at the context. Some Bible translators attempted to translate *sarx* into what they thought it meant in that particular context, but many got it wrong. Only the translators of the literal translations (e.g. KJV or NKJV and a few others) did not change the word *sarx* into what they thought it might mean, but left it in the English verses simply as "flesh", allowing the reader to interpret the context. That's why Romans 7 and some other passages appear to be so confusing in some translations, because *sarx* (which means "flesh") was replaced with "sinful nature" every time!

Here's an example of where *sarx* was interpreted in two different ways:

> *I want you to know how much I am struggling for you and for those at Laodicea, and for all who have not met me personally* [personally = sarx]. *(Col 2:1 NIV, annotations added)*

> *For I want you to know what a great conflict I have for you and*
> *those in Laodicea, and for as many as have not seen my face in the*
> *flesh* [flesh = sarx]. *(Col 2:1 NKJV, annotations added)*

Spiritual Circumcision

Now when the Bible talks about the "inward man", the "new man" or the "new nature", it speaks about the born again spirit of a believer. The "sinful nature" or "old man" refers to the evil, sinful nature that every person in the earth is born with. This nature is at enmity with God and alive to sin, but it was completely cut out from us the day we became born again:

> *In him you were also circumcised, in the putting off of the sinful*
> *nature, not with a circumcision done by the hands of men but with*
> *the circumcision done by Christ (Col 2:11 NIV).*

Note this is not a physical circumcision, since the verse says "*not with a circumcision done by the hands of men*". It must therefore be a spiritual circumcision, meaning the cutting away or the removal of the sinful nature.

Crucified and Buried with Christ

In Romans 6 Paul uses another image of how our old sinful nature was completely removed. At salvation, a Christian's sinful nature is actually conveyed back through time to the cross and crucified and buried with Christ:

> *...knowing this, that our old man* [sinful nature] *was crucified*
> *with Him, that the body of sin might be done away with, that we*
> *should no longer be slaves of sin. (Rom 6:6 NKJV, annotations*
> *added)*

After we are born again, we are not "sinners" anymore, even though we sometimes make mistakes. There is not one verse in the entire New Covenant that calls a born again believer a "sinner". The term "sinner" refers to a person that has not yet been born again (this is consistent throughout the entire New Testament after the cross) and yet we find most Christians today thinking: "I am just an old sinner."

No we are not!

Under the Old Covenant people had to be circumcised on the eighth day in accordance with the law. Under the New Covenant God circumcises the heart of the believer, removing (cutting out) the old evil nature (see Colossians 2:11 above again) and giving us a new resurrected spirit that is created in 100% perfect righteousness like Christ. God also writes His laws on our hearts which simply means He gives us the desire to please Him (but of course we know He is actually already pleased with us because of what Jesus did on our behalf).

> *For I delight in the law of God according to the inward man.*
> *(Rom 7:22 NKJV)*

This means that our new reborn spirit desires to please God and delights in Him.

The following comparisons between literal and conceptual Bible translations clearly illustrate this misconception. Please note we're not criticizing certain Bible translations, rather we're addressing the misconception in the church about a born again believer's inner nature, as well as the translation of the word *sarx*:

> *...in order that the righteous requirements of the law might be fully met in us, who do not live according to the sinful nature* [sarx] *but according to the Spirit. Those who live according to the sinful nature* [sarx] *have their minds set on what that nature* [sarx] *desires; but those who live in accordance with the Spirit have their minds set on what the Spirit desires. (Rom 8:4-5 NIV, annotations added)*

Now compare:

> *...that the righteous requirement of the law might be fulfilled in us who do not walk according to the flesh* [sarx] *but according to the Spirit. For those who live according to the flesh* [sarx] *set their minds on the things of the flesh* [sarx]*, but those who live according to the Spirit, the things of the Spirit. (Rom 8:4 NKJV, annotations added)*

It is very easy to see from the first example that a believer can be made to believe that they still have a sinful nature on the inside. However from the second example the correct interpretation can be made, namely that believers who set their thoughts on the things of their unrenewed minds (old thought patterns, bad habits, etc), will live to try and gratify those desires and not walk according to the desires of their new born again spirit man. We do not have to battle a sinful nature anymore, the battle is now merely in our minds. Our minds need to be trained (renewed) to line up with the truth of the Word of God.

> *You, my brothers, were called to be free. But do not use your freedom to indulge the sinful nature* [sarx]*; rather, serve one another in love. (Gal 5:13 NIV, annotations added)*

Compare with:

> *For you, brethren, have been called to liberty; only do not use*
> *liberty as an opportunity for the flesh* [sarx], *but through love serve*
> *one another. (Gal 5:13 NKJV, annotations added)*

Since we do not have a sinful nature anymore, we cannot actually indulge in it as mentioned by the first example here. This is a really a no-brainer. Here's another example:

> *So I say, live by the Spirit, and you will not gratify the desires of*
> *the sinful nature* [sarx]. *(Gal 5:16 NIV, annotations added)*

Compare with:

> *I say then: Walk in the Spirit, and you shall not fulfill the lust of*
> *the flesh* [sarx]. *(Gal 5:16 NKJV, annotations added)*

We can't gratify the desires of our sinful nature because we don't have one! However if we train and discipline our minds to line up according to the desires of the born again spirit on the inside, our old habits and thought patterns will begin to starve.

There are many more examples to illustrate this point, but I think we get the idea. Now consider this: The above verses, coupled with the fact that most people today believe whatever they read (without thinking about it) in whatever translation of Bible they have, plus the fact that the modern church has taught for centuries that Christians *do* have a sinful nature (and that we have to deny this sinful nature, fight it tooth and nail and put it to death!), it is easy to see that we can be conned by texts that are read out of context.

Now we may ask: "Why then do Christians still sin? If we don't have a sinful nature, why do we still keep on making mistakes, feeling like we are disappointing God and falling short of what we think God expects from us?" This is what we will be talking about in the next chapter.

In closing, we need to ask ourselves this question: Has God left us with a remnant of our old, evil nature (which would mean He did an incomplete job), or did He do a complete work and remove the whole thing?

Law →✝→ Grace

Why do Christians Sin? Pt 1 (Unrenewed Mind)

In the previous chapter we proved from scripture that God has completely removed our sinful nature when we were born again. God *completely* changed us when we came into salvation; we are brand spanking new!

> *Therefore, if anyone is in Christ, he is a new creation; old things have passed away; behold, all things have become new. (2 Cor 5:17 NKJV)*

Is our body gone? No. Is our mind gone? No. But the above verse definitely says that something "old" has passed away! It is our old spirit man, the sinful nature (indwelling sin) that was completely removed and replaced with a righteous, born again spirit that was created perfect in the image of Christ.

> *...and that you put on the new man which was created according to God, in true righteousness and holiness. (Eph 4:24 NKJV)*

Now the question poses: If God completely removed our sinful nature, why then do we still make mistakes? Why do we still do things that seem contrary to this Godly nature that was birthed in us? The answer is two-fold and we will discuss it over these next two chapters:

1) Because of our unrenewed minds (this chapter)

2) Because of external temptations / distractions (next chapter)

Unrenewed Mind

When we were born into this world with a fallen, sinful nature that was at enmity with God, we lived according to this nature, fulfilling its lusts. When this sinful nature (also called the "old man" in the Bible) told us to commit sin, we did it.

> *Sin came into the world through one man, and his sin brought*
> *death with it. As a result, death has spread to the whole human*
> *race because everyone has sinned. (Rom 5:12 GNB)*

We had no desire to please God and as a result our minds were trained to obey the desires of this sinful nature, with our body simply running after what our mind told it to do. The sinful nature can be seen as the "control room", the driving force behind our decision making. And the mind (soul) was then trained and became accustomed to operating in whichever mannerisms and habits the old sinful nature exercised over it. Our minds were therefore trained and programmed in sin, lustfulness, self preservation and unbelief and we learnt all sorts of bad habits.

Then at salvation, when our sinful nature was completely removed (when we were born again), God gave us a completely new, fully righteous spirit man on the inside, created 100% in the image of Christ, with all of Christ's righteousness and virtue.

Now suddenly our mind (soul) realizes there is a new "control room" on the inside, but it appears as though this new "control room" operates in an entirely different way than the old one. And that's why it sometimes feels as though there is a war raging inside of us, with the mind battling against our new inner man, namely the born again spirit. For years and years the mind (soul) was trained in a certain way and now the new man has to train the mind to operate in a different way.

Previously we spoke about the Greek word *sarx* (which means "flesh") that has different meanings in different contexts. Let's look at its context in the following scripture:

> *I say then: Walk in the Spirit, and you shall not fulfill the lust of*
> *the flesh [sarx]. For the flesh [sarx] lusts against the Spirit, and the*
> *Spirit against the flesh [sarx]; and these are contrary to one another,*
> *so that you do not do the things that you wish. But if you are led by*
> *the Spirit, you are not under the law. Now the works of the flesh*
> *[sarx] are evident, which are: adultery, fornication, uncleanness,*
> *lewdness, idolatry, sorcery, hatred, contentions, jealousies, outbursts*
> *of wrath, selfish ambitions, dissensions, heresies, envy, murders,*
> *drunkenness, revelries. (Gal 5:16-22 NKJV, annotations added)*

Paul wrote this letter to the Galatians, who were born again believers, thus they did not have a sinful nature anymore. Bearing in mind what we have discussed above, it can clearly be seen that in this context, the word "flesh" (sarx) simply means the unrenewed mind (it cannot mean "sinful nature" since we established previously that Christians don't have a sinful nature anymore). Paul was saying that all these lusts were simply works of the believers' unrenewed minds. An unrenewed mind is wired to operate as though the person still has an old sinful nature, even though they haven't.

Directly after the verses above, Paul then contrasts the *works* of the flesh by listing the very well known *fruit* of the spirit:

> *But the fruit of the Spirit is love, joy, peace, longsuffering, kindness, goodness, faithfulness, gentleness, self-control. (Gal 5:22-23 NKJV)*

These are also called the fruit of the Holy Spirit, but actually our born again spirit and the Holy Spirit are joined together, so these can also be seen as the fruit of our born again spirit.

> *But he who is joined to the Lord is one spirit with Him. (1 Cor 6:17 NKJV)*

When we do these good things, they are only a *fruit* of the 100% righteous new spirit man that is inside of us; we don't do them to try and please God or to be more holy, because we are already 100% holy on the inside!

Therefore it can clearly be seen that if our mind is unrenewed, it is at war with our born again spirit and this is simply one of the reasons why we read the Bible, go to church, pray, worship, etc, namely to renew our minds; *not* to earn God's acceptance, because God is already pleased with us. How can He not be if we were created in the very image of His Son Jesus?

This concludes the first reason why Christians still do things which the law calls sin (even though we don't have a sinful nature anymore), namely because of an unrenewed mind. Next we'll deal with the second reason: External temptations.

Law →✝→ Grace

Why do Christians Sin? Pt 2 (External Temptations)

Previously we established from scripture that born again Christians don't have a sinful nature anymore. We also talked about one of the reasons why believers, even though they no longer have a sinful nature, still sin, namely because of an unrenewed mind. In this chapter we will talk about the second reason: external temptations.

Many people still have the idea that after Christians are born again, they still have a part of that old, evil, sinful nature inside them and that they have to live everyday trying to kill that evil nature with its desires, fighting it tooth and nail, hoping to somehow eventually reach a place where they can feel they have behaved good enough to be able to approach God with confidence.

This misconception is often prompted by verses such as these:

> Therefore do not let sin reign in your mortal body so that you obey its _evil_ desires. (Rom 6:12 NIV, emphasis added)

> ...but each one is tempted when, by his own _evil_ desire, he is dragged away and enticed. (Jam 1:14 NIV, emphasis added)

The word "evil" does not appear in the original language in either of these verses, but was inserted by the translators, who were trying to interpret a concept (they were convinced that Christians still had a sinful nature), rather than allowing the readers to interpret the context themselves. A true born again believer is not evil anymore; we have a 100% holy and righteous spirit man living on the inside of us that wants to please God in everything it does. But we still stumble sometimes because of our unrenewed mind (soul), which was trained to think and operate the way it does by years of conditioning and suffering under the control of our old evil sinful nature. Thus the above two verses make more sense when we read it out of a literal translation (note the word "evil" has been omitted):

> *Therefore do not let sin reign in your mortal body, that you should obey it in its lusts. (Rom 6:12 NKJV)*

> *But each one is tempted when he is drawn away by his own desires and enticed. (Jam 1:14 NKJV)*

"If Christians could flick a switch that would enable them to stop sinning immediately and walk in obedience 100% of the time, they would flick that switch in a heartbeat" (Ryan Rufus - City Church International, Hong Kong). The children of God *want* to please God and live holy because their new spirit man has the desire to please God. But sometimes we do not walk according to this spirit man and we mess up. But we can be confident that when we sin, there is always an abundance of grace to cover that sin!

> *Moreover the law entered that the offense might abound. But where sin abounded, grace abounded much more. (Rom 5:20 NKJV)*

God knew our minds would not be renewed in a heartbeat and that we would always, until we go on to be with Him in heaven, struggle with some form of sin (either in our minds, thought patterns, attitudes) and therefore He took the sin "problem" out of the way completely at the cross by pouring out His *full* indignation against sin on the Lamb. Jesus bore the full brunt of the punishment for our sins.

A second reason why Christians keep on doing things that the law calls "sin" (even though they don't have a sinful nature anymore) is because of external temptations. Temptation appeals to our body and soul (mind), but not to our born again spirit man. The body will follow like a slave to whichever one of these two we yield control to.

> *For he who sows to his flesh will of the flesh reap corruption, but he who sows to the Spirit will of the Spirit reap everlasting life. (Gal 6:8 NKJV)*

This verse simply means that when our unrenewed mind lusts after some carnal thing and we yield our body to it, the body will be a slave to sin and reap the earthly consequences of that sin. Yes *earthly* consequences, because all the eternal consequences (the punishment) were dealt with at the cross. But if we walk according to the desires of our new inner spirit man, the body will be a slave to righteousness and reap the benefits, both temporal and eternal.

Another great advantage of walking after the spirit includes having our mind (soul) transformed. The mind can be affected and influenced (trained) by the spirit to learn obedience, but the spirit can never be influenced by the mind because it has been made 100% righteous by God and can never be corrupted – it's a one way street only. The Bible says that our born again spirit has been "fused" with the Holy Spirit, they have become one (1 Corinthians 6:17). If it were possible for our soul to corrupt our born again spirit, then it would mean that the Holy Spirit can be corrupted because He is one with our spirit.

However a believer's born again spirit can be suppressed if they choose to walk after the lusts of the unrenewed mind. It all comes down to a choice. But the choice is not really that hard if we consider the glorious riches we have in Him, seeing that we are seated with Christ in heavenly places, feeling His loving presence on us and having wave upon wave of grace rush over us every day. What depths of love are contained in the God we serve!

Law →✝→ Grace

Divorced from the Law

Therefore, my brethren, you also have become dead to the law through the body of Christ, that you may be married to another - to Him who was raised from the dead, that we should bear fruit to God. (Rom 7:4 NKJV)

This verse says that we have to die to the law in order for us to bear fruit. This implies that if we have not yet died to the law, we cannot actually bear fruit. But what is fruit? It is the result of the Holy Spirit living through us (Galatians 5:22-23), the very manifestations of His character and not our own efforts to try and live holy. That's why it is called "fruit". But instead of letting the Holy Spirit live through us, we suppress Him when we try to do enough stuff for God so that He can approve of us.

This is a pattern in the life of most Christians who live under the law: One week they'd have a good week, feeling that they didn't make too many mistakes and that God is pleased with them. But then they'd find themselves doing that one thing they swore they'd never do again and they're back to square one.

The law demands a level of obedience that no human being is able to achieve and failure to comply is punishable by death. But that's where Jesus comes in: He lived a perfect sinless life, fulfilling *all* the requirements of the law (Matthew 5:17-18) thereby effectively *ending* it:

> *For Christ is the <u>end of the law</u> for righteousness to everyone who believes. (Rom 10:4 NKJV, emphasis added)*

He destroyed the hold of sin (which was strengthened by the law) by removing the punishment for sin completely:

> *The sting of death is sin, and <u>the strength of sin is the law</u>. (1 Cor 15:56 NKJV, emphasis added)*

Andre van der Merwe

He set us at liberty to live free from the fear of judgment (1 John 4:17-18) and the power of sin:

> *For sin shall not have dominion over you, for you are not under law but under grace. (Rom 6:14 NKJV)*

This explains why so many people are struggling with sin in their lives - because they are trying to live under the law and not under grace!

God Made a Vow

When two people marry they make a vow to stay true to each other until death should part them. Now back in the old days when a person's vow still actually meant something, a vow could not be broken except through death by one of the parties involved. Now the same goes for vows / covenants / oaths made by God. When God makes a vow, it *will* come to pass! So when God made a covenant with Israel and gave them the 10 Commandments and the Old Covenant Law, the only way for them to be able to get out of that covenant was to fulfill it or to die for violating it.

Now watch this: Jesus Christ fulfilled the law *as a man*, thereby upholding man's side of the covenant and earning all the blessings on our behalf. But because we couldn't uphold our part, He then went even further and tasted death for us as well, carrying all the curses and punishment for disobedience on our behalf. Now if that isn't love, what is?

Now by simply putting our faith in Jesus we also die to the law and consequently to all the curses for disobeying the law. We become alive to God and through Christ are given *all* the blessings for His obedience:

> *Blessed (be) the God and Father of our Lord Jesus Christ, who has blessed us with every spiritual blessing in the Heavenly (places) in Christ. (Eph 1:3 NKJV)*

We have died to the law and we are now married to another husband, namely Jesus Christ!

> *Or do you not know, brethren (for I speak to those who know the law), that the law has dominion over a man as long as he lives? For the woman who has a husband is bound by the law to her husband as long as he lives. But if the husband dies, she is released from the law of her husband. So then if, while her husband lives, she marries another man, she will be called an adulteress; but if her husband dies, she is free from that law, so that she is no adulteress,*

though she has married another man. Therefore, my brethren, you also have become dead to the law through the body of Christ, that you may be married to another - to Him who was raised from the dead, that we should bear fruit to God. (Rom 7:1-4 NKJV)

For I through the law died to the law that I might live to God. (Gal 2:19 NKJV)

Once we realize that we are actually dead to the Old Covenant Law, we will stop trying to relate to God on the basis of our own good or bad behavior and simply love Him because He is a good Dad. Gone are the days of do's and don'ts; of running around like slaves to try and live up to the demands of the old husband of the law, that slaps us around and always demands more! Here are the days of being married to our new husband, Jesus Christ, who loves us because we are His glorious bride, His beloved church. Yay God!

Law →✝→ Grace

Tithes and Offerings

Cain and Abel were the first record in the entire Bible of someone bringing an offering to God. Remember this was long before the law and the 10 Commandments had ever been introduced. There was no stipulation that demanded they should give anything to God or to the church, because the church didn't even exist yet. They gave God an offering simply out of their free will.

Abraham

In Genesis 14 we have the first record of someone actually "tithing" in the Bible, and then he didn't even tithe from out of his own possessions, but gave a tenth of the spoils from a battle he'd just won. Abraham had just defeated the four kings with his 318 men:

> When Abram came back from his victory over Chedorlaomer and the other kings, the king of Sodom went out to meet him in Shaveh Valley (also called King's Valley). And Melchizedek, who was king of Salem and also a priest of the Most High God, brought bread and wine to Abram, blessed him, and said, "May the Most High God, who made Heaven and earth, bless Abram! May the Most High God, who gave you victory over your enemies, be praised!" And Abram gave Melchizedek a tenth of all the loot he had recovered. (Gen 14:17-20 GNB)

There was no person nor any law that forced Abraham to tithe, because the laws of Moses were only introduced 430 years later:

> What I mean is that God made a covenant with Abraham and promised to keep it. The Law, which was given four hundred and thirty years later, cannot break that covenant and cancel God's promise. (Gal 3:17 GNB)

Many preachers say that because Abraham gave a tithe before the law, it serves as a type and a shadow of what believers under the New Covenant (who are also not under the law) should also do. Bertie Brits from Dynamic Love Ministries[1] makes a very interesting observation regarding Abraham's tithe:

"Long before the law was given, Abraham tithed, animals were sacrificed and people were circumcised. Can we therefore say that because Abraham tithed before the law, people were circumcised or because animals were sacrificed, that we should do the same today? Of course not! It doesn't matter which way we look at it, we can not make Abraham's action into a command for believers under the New Covenant."

Another interesting point to note was that Abraham gave 10% of the loot he had just won from a war! He also only did it once! It's therefore not accurate to assume that what Abraham did serves as an example for us to give away 10% of our income every month.

Jacob

Jacob was instructed by his father (Isaac) to go from Canaan, to Padanaram and the house of Laban (his mother's brother) to take for himself a wife. One night on the way there, he fell asleep and dreamt about the angels of the Lord ascending and descending on a great ladder that extended down from heaven onto the earth. God reaffirmed the vow He had made to Abraham, to bless him and make him into a great nation. After Jacob had woken up, he built an altar and called the place *Bethel*, because the Lord was in that place. Then he said this:

> *Then Jacob made a vow, saying, "If God will be with me, and keep me in this way that I am going, and give me bread to eat and clothing to put on, so that I come back to my father's house in peace, then the LORD shall be my God. And this stone which I have set as a pillar shall be God's house, <u>and of all that You give me I will surely give a tenth to You</u>". (Gen 28:20-22 NKJV, emphasis added)*

Jacob did not think: "I'd better give ten percent to God else He's not going to bless me". No! Jacob already knew he was blessed because God had just made a vow to bless him. He knew that God would take care of him and *because* he expected to be laden with wealth by God, he said that he'd give back ten percent of all he received from God.

This flies straight in the face of most church doctrines today. Just about everywhere we go it is preached that we need to give to God first if we want to receive anything from Him. "You cannot receive if you have not given anything!" is proclaimed far and wide. Well this is definitely not the way it would appear from the above scriptures in Genesis 28. Jacob said that he would only give *after* God had given to him first.

"Encouraged" to Give

Because so many ministries these days are facing financial difficulties, they often "encourage" their members to "give" generously to the work of the Lord. Unfortunately most of the time the Bible verses used and the motives given are law based. Note the following saying: "If it's God's will, it's God's bill. If He leads He feeds".

If a ministry were really commissioned by God and the people established in grace, the leadership would never have to preach on tithing because the members would automatically give out of a motive of love. They would feel they are actually contributing towards something significant and not feel they *have* to give just to help their ministry's struggling cause. When God really commissions a ministry He always provides for that ministry and its people supernaturally. God equips the called.

The Malachi 3 Manipulation Method

Teaching people to tithe out of Malachi 3 is Old Covenant Law! Remember that the entire Bible was written *for* us, but not everything in the Bible was written directly *to* us. This section of the prophetic book of Malachi was written specifically to the nation of Israel who was still living under the Old Covenant Law and had at the time turned away from God.

The following is a short extract from <u>Matthew Henry's Concise Commentary on the Book of Malachi</u>: *Malachi was the last of the Old Testament prophets, and is supposed to have prophesied B.C. 420. He reproves the priests and the people for the evil practices into which they had fallen, and invites them to repentance and reformation, with promises of the blessings to be bestowed at the coming of the Messiah.*

Malachi was rebuking the nation of <u>Israel</u> for forsaking God and not keeping the law of Moses, which included tithing. And what were the results of breaking these laws? Curse upon curse (see Deut 28:15 onwards). But we know that we are not under the Law of Moses and its curses anymore, because Christ became a curse for us (Galatians 3:13). Now with this in the back our minds, let's read these often misunderstood verses:

> *For I am the LORD, I do not change; Therefore you are not consumed, <u>O sons of Jacob</u>* [Malachi is addressing Israel]. *Yet from*

the days of your fathers <u>you have gone away from My ordinances</u> <u>and have not kept them</u> [Israel is being rebuked for not obeying the commandments - this is the context!]. Return to Me, and I will return to you," says the LORD of hosts.

"But you said, 'In what way shall we return?' "Will a man rob God? Yet you have robbed Me! But you say, 'In what way have we robbed You?'

In tithes and offerings. You are cursed with a curse, for you have robbed Me, even this whole nation. Bring all the tithes into the storehouse, that there may be food in My house, and try Me now in this," says the LORD of hosts, "If I will not open for you the windows of heaven and pour out for you such blessing that there will not be room enough to receive it. "And I will rebuke the devourer for your sakes, so that he will not destroy the fruit of your ground, nor shall the vine fail to bear fruit for you in the field," says the LORD of hosts. (Mal 3:6-11 NKJV, annotations and emphasis added)

There are actually quite a few clues that make it crystal clear this is Old Covenant:

First Clue

"Return to Me, and I will return to you," says the LORD of hosts. (Mal 3:7b NKJV)

Under the New Covenant God promised to never leave or forsake us:

...and lo, I am with you always, even to the end of the age." Amen. (Matt 28:20b NKJV)

Second Clue

You are cursed with a curse, for you have robbed Me, even this whole nation. (Mal 3:9 NKJV)

Under the New Covenant Jesus Christ became a curse for us so that we would never have to bear any of the curses for disobeying the Old Covenant Laws, including tithing:

> *Christ redeemed us from the curse of the Law, being made a curse for us (for it is written, "Cursed is everyone having been hanged on a tree"). (Gal 3:13 NKJV)*

There are more clues, but I think we get the picture. To get to the point, often verse 10 is used by preachers to "encourage" people to give and to "test" God's faithfulness:

Bring all the tithes into the storehouse, that there may be food in My house, and try Me now in this," says the LORD of hosts, "If I will not open for you the windows of heaven and pour out for you such blessing that there will not be room enough to receive it.

This is law based preaching again because this teaches that *only if* people do their part *then* God will do His part. But actually God has already proven His love and faithfulness towards us:

> *But God has shown us how much he loves us - it was while we were still sinners that Christ died for us! (Rom 5:8 GNB)*

In fact God never has to do a single thing again to prove Himself faithful, because He has already given his most treasured gift: His own Son!

And here is the most ironic phenomenon: When people are recommended to "test" God's faithfulness, they are normally also given the bank account details or very conveniently told where they can deposit this money with which they intend to "test" God...

Don't Call it Tithing!

What we should really be doing is to not even call it "tithing" in the first place, because "tithing" refers to the giving of an exact amount of money (10% percent of our income), turning it into a stipulation or law again. If believers wish to give money to the work of the Lord, they are commanded to do so cheerfully:

> *So let each one give as he purposes in his heart, not grudgingly or of necessity; for God loves a cheerful giver. (2 Cor 9:7 NKJV)*

If giving 10% of their income does not make someone cheerful, then they shouldn't give at all! If giving 5% or 40% or even 1% of their income is what makes them cheerful, then that is what they should give. In the end, whatever a person chooses to give, it's all about their motive. If somebody isn't giving anything at all and they do so cheerfully, then that is their choice: they shouldn't give just because they feel the need to give, read 2 Corinthians 9:7 again. So let's not call it "tithing" but instead call it "giving".

So in the light of the New Covenant, where then does "giving" fit in? The answer is two-fold:

1.   The first part of this answer relates to our positional standing with God; our identity in Him: Giving fits in exactly where holy living, obedience and loving other people fit in - it is something that happens simply because of who we are. Our inner nature (or our born again spirit) is now holy and set apart unto God. Good works is something that just flows out from us as naturally as breathing.

      There is no effort or striving, but simply rest and a motive of returning love to the One who loved us first. His love for us is so complete that nothing we do can ever make Him love or accept us more. And if He cannot love us anymore than He already does, then giving money to the church to earn His love really becomes meaningless and perverted, just like all other works of self righteousness.

2.   Secondly this answer relates to the natural realm, to our physical lives and the expansion of God's kingdom here in the earth. God made the earth in such a way that almost everything functions by means of money. Therefore in order to mobilize missionaries, maintain infrastructure, resource evangelists, etc. the church needs financial resources to function. Paul preached that people who put their lives into spreading the gospel should also be able to live off the gospel:

      My defense to those who examine me is this: Do we have no right to eat and drink? Do we have no right to take along a believing wife, as do also the other apostles, the brothers of the Lord, and Cephas? Or is it only Barnabas and I who have no right to refrain from working? Who ever goes to war at his own expense? Who plants a vineyard and does not eat of its fruit? Or who tends a flock and does not drink of the milk of the flock? Do I say these things as a mere man? Or does not the law say the same also? For it is written in the law of Moses, "You shall not muzzle an ox while it treads out the grain." Is it oxen God is concerned about? Or does He say it altogether for our sakes? For our sakes, no doubt, this is written, that he who plows should plow in hope, and he who threshes in hope should be partaker of his hope. If we have sown spiritual things for you, is it a great thing if we reap your material things? If others are partakers of this right over you, are we not even more? Nevertheless we have not used this right, but endure all things lest we hinder the gospel of Christ. Do you not know that those who minister the holy things eat of the things of the temple, and those

> *who serve at the altar partake of the offerings of the altar? Even so*
> *the Lord has commanded that those who preach the gospel should*
> *live from the gospel. (1 Cor 9:3-14 NKJV)*

And because this is true then it means that those who draw benefit from the message (the hearers) have a responsibility to care for the needs of the ones who are bringing the message. But even so, the most important thing is that it should *still* be out of a motive of love and a cheerful heart. Believers are not supposed to be manipulated into giving for whatever reason. The amount we give should be "as we purpose in our hearts" as we have read in 2 Corinthians 9:7 (above). There are churches where people are "motivated" to give so much to the church that they take out second mortgages on their homes, while the pastor spends luxury holidays on his yacht. Come on! We didn't give up our right to think logically when we became Christians; clearly there is something wrong with this picture!

The flip side to this story is that the apostle Paul, even though he may have had some sort of right to claim financial support from the churches, did not make use of it. The gifts that he received from some of the churches were given out of love, because the people had a concern for Paul's wellbeing.

> *Did you get less of me or of God than any of the other churches? The*
> *only thing you got less of was less responsibility for my upkeep. Well,*
> *I'm sorry. Forgive me for depriving you. Everything is in readiness*
> *now for this, my third visit to you. But don't worry about it; you*
> *won't have to put yourselves out. I'll be no more of a bother to you*
> *this time than on the other visits. I have no interest in what you*
> *have - only in you. <u>Children shouldn't have to look out for their*
> *parents; parents look out for the children. I'd be most happy to*
> *empty my pockets, even mortgage my life, for your good.</u> So how*
> *does it happen that the more I love you, the less I'm loved? And why*
> *is it that I keep coming across these whiffs of gossip about how <u>my*
> *self-support</u> was a front behind which I worked an elaborate scam?*
> *Where's the evidence? Did I cheat or trick you through anyone I*
> *sent? I asked Titus to visit, and sent some brothers along. Did they*
> *swindle you out of anything? And haven't we always been just as*
> *aboveboard, just as honest? I hope you don't think that all along*
> *we've been making our defense before you, the jury. You're not the*
> *jury; God is the jury - God revealed in Christ - and we make our*
> *case before him. And we've gone to all the trouble of supporting*
> *ourselves so that we won't be in the way or get in the way of your*
> *growing up. (2 Cor 12:13-19 MSG, emphasis added)*

It's a heartrending reality that the majority of the people involved in leadership roles in churches across the world do not have Paul's shepherd heart for their flock, but instead see their flock as a means to sustain themselves and build their own empires.

Paul also clearly mentioned that he was supporting *himself* in these passages, so to see Paul's words in 1 Corinthians 9 (above) as a rule that preachers should earn an income off those who benefit from their message, is entirely incorrect. If Paul did establish this as a rule, why was he then breaking his own rules?

Where to Give

Where should we give? In the Old Testament people had to bring their tithes and offerings to the temple. But since God doesn't live in manmade buildings anymore (like He did in the Old Testament) but in the temples of our human bodies, it cannot really be argued that we should give our money to support the institution which calls itself the "church" anymore, because in the New Covenant WE ARE the church. However when we find a person or ministry who contributes to our spiritual wellbeing, it's really not much of a sacrifice to give them money, is it? It actually becomes a privilege, a partnership, a faith motivated gesture of love. When we sow into a ministry that produces life and bears fruit, we become partakers and partners of that life because we have sown into it and the Word teaches that every seed brings forth fruit after its own kind (Genesis 1:11).

Offerings can also be given to people or ministries which we believe are making a difference in the world in reaching the unsaved and getting the gospel to the nations. Alms are also given to the poor and needy to the extent we are able to. The Bible further models giving to apostolic fathers (like the churches that sent offerings to the apostle Paul to support him, see Philippians 4:14-17) and living a lifestyle of generosity and sharing (Acts 4:32-36 and also 1 Timothy 6:17-18).

On the other hand when we are sowing into a ministry that is promoting law motivated living (that teaches God will not bless us if we don't tithe, or where we are constantly made to feel guilty about our lifestyle or about this and that sin or for not giving enough), we are sowing into a ministry that produces death, since the Bible calls the law a ministry of death (2 Corinthians 3:7). We needn't worry however that we will reap death or curse from such a ministry because Christ became a curse for us according to Galatians 3:13. However we will not reap spiritual life from this ministry either since they are not producing any life. Even though the works they do may appear to be helping others, a pattern that normally emerges in these ministries is that things are so well organized and arranged that they seem to manage fairly well on their own – they don't actually seem to need God. They don't need to trust God for anything since they manage to extract pretty much all they need from their people using their calculated, manipulative methods.

It is always best to sow into the place where we are spiritually fed and where life is imparted to us; the place where we can see that people are being saved and healed and the Kingdom is expanded.

We can trust that God is always good and that He will always bless and love us, regardless if we give our entire salary away or if we don't give a cent. Will God not love and bless us the same and even more than He does the lilies in the field and the birds in the air that don't even give Him anything...?

Law →✝→ Grace

Job

This often misquoted, misunderstood book in the Bible has been the cause of much blame to fall on God for causing sickness, poverty, despair, loss of loved ones and suffering. In fact it's almost strange if any Christian has not at some point in their life blamed God for something bad that's happened to them, thinking: "If He allowed it to happen to Job, He'll allow it to happen to me".

According to theologians, the book of Job is probably the oldest book in the Bible, written even before Moses recorded Genesis to Deuteronomy. Job was an upright and God fearing man:

> *There was a man in the land of Uz, whose name was Job; and that man was blameless and upright, and one who feared God and shunned evil. (Job 1:1 NKJV)*

Since the law and 10 Commandments had not yet been introduced, there was no standard of holiness to try and measure up to and Job had free and open access to God's presence. Then one day the following happened:

> *Now there was a day when the sons of God came to present themselves before the LORD, and Satan also came among them. And the LORD said to Satan, "From where do you come?" So Satan answered the LORD and said, "From going to and fro on the earth, and from walking back and forth on it". (Job 1:6-7 NKJV)*

How did Satan ever manage to get to heaven and appear before God? This is a topic we will look at in depth in our next two chapters.

The point is, even *if* Satan could at one point manage to stand in heaven before God, he can't do it any longer. Shortly after Jesus had sent out the seventy disciples, they came back to Him, rejoicing that even demons were subject to His name:

> *Then the seventy returned with joy, saying, "Lord, even the demons are subject to us in Your name." And He said to them, "I saw Satan fall like lightning from Heaven. (Luk 10:17-18 NKJV)*

Satan was cast out from heaven (again) on that day! He no longer had any right to stand before God and accuse mankind of anything! Therefore we do not have to fear that Satan can report any bad conduct to God anymore. It has all been forgiven at the cross.

Job and His Friends Accuse God

During the period that Satan tried to destroy Job, things were made even worse by Job's friends who came and reasoned with him, trying to share their "wisdom". We saw in Job 1:1 that Job was a righteous man, but now Eliphaz accused him of being sinful and that his suffering was because of his iniquity:

> *"Remember now, who ever perished being innocent? Or where were the upright ever cut off? Even as I have seen, those who plow iniquity and sow trouble reap the same. (Job 4:7-8 NKJV)*

Job himself also accused God of quite a few atrocious things:

> *God throws me into a pit with filth, and even my clothes are ashamed of me. If God were human, I could answer him; we could go to court to decide our quarrel. But there is no one to step between us - no one to judge both God and me. Stop punishing me, God! Keep your terrors away! (Job 9:31-34 GNB)*

Job claimed that God was responsible for killing him, yet he maintained he would still trust God. This sounds quite a bit like those who accuse God for killing their children or loved ones, but say they still "trust" Him. Come on! If God were responsible for doing such things, why would people even still want to be Christians? How can we trust someone that murders our loved ones?

> *Though He slay me, yet will I trust Him. (Job 13:15a NKJV)*

God Has His Say

In the end, after going around in circles many times and having the issue even more confused by his three so called friends, God steps in and speaks to Job from within a violent storm:

And now, finally, GOD answered Job from the eye of a violent storm. He said: "Why do you confuse the issue? Why do you talk without knowing what you're talking about? Pull yourself together, Job! Up on your feet! Stand tall! I have some questions for you, and I want some straight answers. (Job 38:1-3 MSG)

God then goes on to describe the spectacular ways in which He created the universe, including animals, the oceans and the heavens and asks Job if he were ever present when these things were created. In the end Job realizes the error of his ways and his foolish words and he becomes too distressed to speak:

Job answered: "I'm speechless, in awe - words fail me. I should never have opened my mouth! I've talked too much, way too much. I'm ready to shut up and listen." (Job 40:3-5 MSG)

You asked, 'Who is this who hides counsel without knowledge?' Therefore I have uttered what I did not understand, things too wonderful for me, which I did not know. (Job 42:3 NKJV, emphasis added)

Now if we can forget about being religious and think logically for a moment: If somebody were to talk about things they did not understand, what are they actually doing? They are talking rubbish! Job was talking rubbish! He even admitted it several times! We can therefore, like Job, not accuse God for punishing us, allowing difficulty in our lives, stealing from us or anything of the like since we would be talking rubbish.

Our Father is a good God and a giver of good things:

Every good gift and every perfect gift is from above, and comes down from the Father of lights, with whom there is no variation or shadow of turning. (Jam 1:17 NKJV)

If anybody claims they are going through a "Job experience" but they do not come out twice as rich and blessed on the other side, then they've not really experienced what Job went through, but instead felt firsthand what it's like to be robbed by the devil:

The thief does not come except to steal, and to kill, and to destroy. I have come that they may have life, and that they may have it more abundantly. (John 10:10 NKJV)

These are the only two job descriptions in the Bible - it's up to us to decide who is responsible for which...

Law →✝→ Grace

The Origin of the Devil

The devil (Lucifer) was created as the main angel (cherub) of music in heaven and he held that position until iniquity was found in him. When the prophet Ezekiel wrote about the king of Tyre, he was actually referring to Satan – this was a type of figurative speech used when talking about someone while actually referring to somebody else. We know Ezekiel was talking about the devil because apart from God, there were only three other people in the Garden of Eden: Adam, Eve and Satan talking through the snake. Note how beautifully Lucifer had been created:

> Moreover the word of the LORD came to me, saying, "Son of man, take up a lamentation for the king of Tyre, and say to him, 'Thus says the Lord GOD: "You were the seal of perfection, full of wisdom and perfect in beauty. You were in Eden, the garden of God; every precious stone was your covering: The sardius, topaz, and diamond, beryl, onyx, and jasper, sapphire, turquoise, and emerald with gold. The workmanship of your timbrels and pipes was prepared for you on the day you were created. "You were the anointed cherub who covers; I established you; you were on the holy mountain of God; You walked back and forth in the midst of fiery stones. You were perfect in your ways from the day you were created, till iniquity was found in you. "By the abundance of your trading you became filled with violence within, and you sinned; Therefore I cast you as a profane thing out of the mountain of God; and I destroyed you, O covering cherub, from the midst of the fiery stones. "Your heart was lifted up because of your beauty; you corrupted your wisdom for the sake of your splendor; I cast you to the ground, I laid you before kings, that they might gaze at you. "You defiled your sanctuaries by the multitude of your iniquities, by the iniquity of your trading; therefore I brought fire from your

midst; it devoured you, and I turned you to ashes upon the earth in the sight of all who saw you. All who knew you among the peoples are astonished at you; you have become a horror, and shall be no more for ever."". (Eze 28:12-19 NKJV)

Lucifer (which means "Angel of Light") was corrupted because of his own beauty and he became full of pride. Through some form of cunning negotiation or scheme (the above verses point out that he was "trading") he managed to corrupt many of the angels in heaven as well. And since sin cannot exist in heaven, he was cast out and these angels with him:

And there was war in Heaven. Michael and his angels warring against the dragon. And the dragon and his angels warred, but did not prevail. Nor was place found for them in Heaven any more. And the great dragon was cast out, the old serpent called Devil, and Satan, who deceives the whole world. He was cast out into the earth, and his angels were cast out with him. (Rev 12:7-9 NKJV)

The devil was now the ruler of the earth, since he was cast down there from heaven. Then God created man and placed him on the earth and instructed him to cultivate and guard the Garden of Eden.

Then the LORD God placed the man in the Garden of Eden to cultivate it and guard it. (Gen 2:15 GNB)

What did man have to guard it against, after all, the lion and the lamb still grazed together? Against Satan of course! The devil had ruled the earth until then, but now God had placed man on the earth to rule in Satan's place:

And God blessed them. And God said to them, Be fruitful, and multiply and fill the earth, and subdue it. And have dominion over the fish of the sea and over the fowl of the Heavens, and all animals that move upon the earth. (Gen 1:28 NKJV)

Therefore because of God's decree, man was the rightful ruler of the earth.

We then read how through Adam's negligence to guard the earth properly, Satan managed to use the body of a snake to entice Eve, who misled Adam as well. He led them to believe that they would become like God, when in fact they already were!

So God created man in His own image; in the image of God He created him; male and female He created them. (Gen 1:27 NKJV)

They carried God's glory to the extent that they weren't even aware they were naked. But after they had eaten of the forbidden fruit they realized they were naked (actually they realized that God's glory, which had covered them before, had lifted), which really meant they had died spiritually.

Through this single act of disobedience Adam plunged mankind into sin and since the seed of all the people on the earth was still inside him, every person ever born into this world would be born with a sinful nature:

> *Therefore, just as through one man sin entered the world, and death through sin, and thus death spread to all men... (Rom 5:12a NKJV)*

This is why it was necessary for Jesus to be born of a virgin: so that He would not inherit the sinful nature passed on from generation to generation since Adam. Jesus was conceived through God's own seed through the Holy Spirit. This is the very same seed which is given to us when we are born again:

> *...having been born again, not of corruptible seed but incorruptible, through the word of God which lives and abides for ever. (1 Pet 1:23 NKJV)*

Law →✝→ Grace

Defeating the Devil

Through Adam's submission to Satan, he became a slave to Satan's devices and by implication allowed Satan to become ruler of the earth. That which we allow ourselves to be overcome by, becomes our master:

> ...for by whom a person is overcome, by him also he is brought into bondage. (2 Pet 2:19b NKJV)

And also:

> Do you not know that to whom you present yourselves slaves to obey, you are that one's slaves whom you obey, whether of sin leading to death, or of obedience leading to righteousness? (Rom 6:16 NKJV)

This is how Satan managed to stand in heaven before God in the book of Job:

> Now there was a day when the sons of God came to present themselves before the LORD, and Satan also came among them. And the LORD said to Satan, "From where do you come?" So Satan answered the LORD and said, "From going to and fro on the earth, and from walking back and forth on it". (Job 1:6-7 NKJV)

Adam was a son of God, but through his act of disobedience surrendered that position of authority to Satan, who legally became the ruler of this world as even conceded by Jesus:

> I will no longer talk much with you, for the ruler of this world is coming, and he has nothing in Me. (John 14:30 NKJV)

The devil tried the same tactics with Jesus as he did with Adam. Remember how Satan made Adam and Eve question whether they were *really* like God, when in fact they were *already* created in God's image?

> *For God knows that in the day you eat of it your eyes will be opened, <u>and you will be like God</u>, knowing good and evil. (Gen 3:5 NKJV, emphasis added)*

In exactly the same way Satan asked Jesus *if* He was the Son of God during Jesus' forty days in the desert. But unlike Adam, Jesus knew who He was and what was at stake. He knew He had to come and strip Satan of his authority as ruler of the earth.

Because Satan was the ruler of earth's kingdoms, he could legally entice Jesus to worship him and promise Jesus the kingdoms of the world in return:

> *Then the devil, taking Him up on a high mountain, showed Him all the kingdoms of the world in a moment of time. And the devil said to Him, "All this authority I will give You, and their glory; for this has been delivered to me, and I give it to whomever I wish. Therefore, if You will worship before me, all will be Yours". (Luk 4:5-7 NKJV)*

Through Adam's disobedience Satan had become the prince of this world and the kingdoms of the world were legally his to give away.

The Victory of the Cross!

But after defeating the devil at the cross and stripping him of his authority, God reappointed man to the highest position as ruler of the earth (the position that Adam had lost), along with giving believers the authority to trample on Satan and his demons:

> *Behold, I give you the authority to trample on serpents and scorpions, and over all the power of the enemy, and nothing shall by any means hurt you. (Luk 10:19 NKJV)*

God even went as far as parading the devil and his fallen angels in a humiliating manner before their enemies:

> *And having disarmed the powers and authorities, he made a public spectacle of them, triumphing over them by the cross. (Col 2:15 NKJV)*

Through Jesus' sacrifice, obedience and consequent death He did what Adam neglected to do: He conquered evil and ruled over the earth, guarding over it and subduing it in the manner God had commanded Adam to do (Genesis 1:28).

Jesus Christ destroyed the works of the devil everywhere as He went, healing the sick, raising the dead, casting out devils and providing for people's physical needs (such as multiplication of food, obtaining tax money from a fish's mouth, etc). As a normal man He portrayed to all mankind what it can look like to live a life fully surrendered to the Holy Spirit. Apart from being born from a virgin, Jesus had no other advantages over any other believer. Even though He was always the divine Son of God, He restrained all His divinity so that everything He did, all the miracles and wonders, He did as a normal man (if a Christian can be called "normal") through the power of the Holy Spirit, just like the rest of us:

> *Let this mind be in you which was also in Christ Jesus, who, being in the form of God, did not consider it robbery to be equal with God, but made Himself of no reputation, taking the form of a bondservant, and coming in the likeness of men. And being found in appearance as a man, He humbled Himself and became obedient to the point of death, even the death of the cross. (Phil 2:5-8 NKJV)*

Jesus became the last Adam; the One who restored mankind's lost authority and restored God's children to unhindered, unbroken fellowship with the Father. Death came through Adam's disobedience, but life came through Christ's obedience.

> *For as in Adam all die, even so in Christ all shall be made alive. (1 Cor 15:22 NKJV)*

> *For as by one man's disobedience many were made sinners, so also by one Man's obedience many will be made righteous. (Rom 5:19 NKJV)*

Why Then is the World So Broken?

Now this naturally poses the following question: If the enemy has already been defeated, why is he still causing so much havoc in the world? Why are there so many wars and diseases; why all the violence and poverty? Why are people suffering and dying by the millions daily?

Because just like Adam, we are not doing our job in guarding the earth properly. The devil was stripped of his authority over 2000 years ago and the only muscle that he now has, is illegal power. The devil can only get away with what we allow him to. He poses as an intimidating and powerful adversary when in fact he has no right to steal, kill and destroy anymore! That is why it is so simple to evict demons and infirmities from people's bodies and lives, because the sound of the Name that destroyed them is enough to make them shiver and leave at once.

Another important factor is that God does not impose His will on mankind. Just like any love relationship between two people can only be truly beautiful when it exists as a result of the free will of both parties, in the same manner God desires for our affection from within our own free will. He did not create dummies or robots to control. If God really wanted to stop Adam from eating that fruit in the Garden of Eden, the Spirit of God inside Adam could have easily smacked the fruit out of Adam's hand. But that would have violated God's permissible will which allows people to make their own free choices.

It is therefore simple to see that God relies on His children to enforce His kingdom in the earth - we are His hands and feet! Let us therefore take up the responsibility which we have been given and rule the earth like we are supposed to. Let's stop this defeated adversary in his tracks and do away with the suffering and harm he causes. Christ in us is the hope of glory!

Law →✝→ Grace

Watered Down Law

In all honesty, those who still choose to live under the Old Covenant Law are actually living according to a "watered down" version. This pertains to *everybody* on the planet who is trying to live according to the law, including even the Jews. The reason for this is because the Old Testament Law, recorded in the first five books of the Bible, contained very specific instructions concerning ritual sacrifices and moral living as well as the punishments for non compliance.

Even if the Jewish temple were to be rebuilt and the ritual animal sacrifices to be reinstated, no person on the planet would ever be justified through their own level of law keeping according to the Bible:

> Therefore <u>by the deeds of the law no flesh will be justified</u> in His sight, for by the law is the knowledge of sin. (Rom 3:20 NKJV, emphasis added)

> Therefore we conclude that a man is justified by faith <u>apart</u> from the deeds of the law. (Rom 3:28 NKJV, emphasis added)

The requirements of the law are actually far more stringent than believed by those who still try to live by it. The biggest problem with trying to live according to the law, is that a person cannot pick and choose which laws they want to obey and which ones not. The law is a composite unity - breaking even the smallest one makes a person guilty of all:

> For whoever shall keep the whole law, and yet stumble in one point, he is guilty of all. For He who said, "Do not commit adultery," also said, "Do not murder." Now if you do not commit adultery, but you do murder, you have become a transgressor of the law. (Jam 2:10-11 NKJV)

Therefore the person found guilty of breaking even the smallest law, like telling a lie, is actually liable for the same punishment as someone who has committed an act of horrific magnitude (like murdering someone). Now who in their right mind wishes to be judged by those standards?

The REAL Standard of the Law

The Mosaic Law was not limited to just the 10 Commandments. After presenting Israel with the two tablets of stone at Mount Sinai, God continued to give Israel a total of 613 laws which they had to keep to the last letter or stand in danger of severe punishment.

Let's take a quick look at some of these laws with the following in mind: Anybody who still argues that Christians have to live according to the Old Testament Laws, but do not practice these things to the last letter themselves, are guilty of disobeying the entire law. Let's take a look at those laws, bearing in mind once again that the Bible is quite a visual book:

> 'If any man has an emission of semen, then he shall wash all his body in water, and be unclean until evening. And any garment and any leather on which there is semen, it shall be washed with water, and be unclean until evening. Also, when a woman lies with a man, and there is an emission of semen, they shall bathe in water, and be unclean until evening. 'If a woman has a discharge, and the discharge from her body is blood, she shall be set apart seven days; and whoever touches her shall be unclean until evening. Everything that she lies on during her impurity shall be unclean; also everything that she sits on shall be unclean. (Lev 15:16-20 NKJV)

Now if people, who claim we still have to live according to the law, don't isolate themselves for seven days during the above circumstances or wash themselves in water after having intercourse, they are guilty of breaking the law and are thereby punishable by death. Here's another one:

> Among the animals, whatever divides the hoof, having cloven hooves and chewing the cud - that you may eat. Nevertheless these you shall not eat among those that chew the cud or those that have cloven hooves: the swine, though it divides the hoof, having cloven hooves, yet does not chew the cud, is unclean to you. (Lev 11:2b, 4, 7 NKJV)

There goes that nice English breakfast with crispy fried bacon.

> *'These you may eat of all that are in the water: whatever in the water has fins and scales, whether in the seas or in the rivers - that you may eat. But all in the seas or in the rivers that do not have fins and scales, all that move in the water or any living thing which is in the water, they are an abomination to you. (Lev 11:9-10 NKJV)*

There goes calamari out the window!

> *And whoever blasphemes the name of the LORD shall surely be put to death. (Lev 24:16a NKJV)*

When last did we see someone stoned for using the Lord's name in vain? Our movies are full of it!

> *"And if a person sins unintentionally, then he shall bring a female goat in its first year as a sin offering." (Num 15:27 NKJV)*

What about all those times we forgot to give to the poor, neglected to give our tithes (because we forgot to bring money to church), washed dishes on the Sabbath, etc? If we didn't go out afterwards, bought a year old female goat and took it to a priest (remember the priest had to be from the correct Jewish lineage) who slaughtered it and made a sin offering for those sins, we've transgressed the law and became guilty of transgressing the entire law. If we were still under the Old Covenant Law, we would be liable for receiving the punishments as per Deuteronomy 28 from verse 15 onwards.

> *Now while the children of Israel were in the wilderness, they found a man gathering sticks on the Sabbath day. And those who found him gathering sticks brought him to Moses and Aaron, and to all the congregation. Then the LORD said to Moses, "The man must surely be put to death; all the congregation shall stone him with stones outside the camp". (Num 15:32-33, 35 NKJV)*

Still want to do those dishes? How about going shopping on the Sabbath?

Ceremonial Law

Another belief doing the rounds among some believers (especially those who believe in tracing back their "Jewish Roots") is that only the ceremonial aspects of the law have ended, but that the legal demands of the law still stand. They argue that all the prescribed rituals in the law have become redundant, but that the law is apparently *still* to be used as a moral guideline to direct our lives and failure to uphold its stipulations will cause us to fall short of God's standards.

Jesus made it clear however that we cannot delete a single letter from the law:

> *For assuredly, I say to you, till Heaven and earth pass away, one jot or one tittle will by no means pass from the law till all is fulfilled. (Matt 5:18 NKJV)*

Another problem with this viewpoint is that none of the ceremonial aspects of the law were *against* us. And the apostle Paul wrote that all the requirements that stood *against* us were cancelled:

> *...by canceling the record of debt that stood <u>against</u> us with its legal demands. This he set aside, nailing it to the cross. (Col 2:14 ESV, emphasis added)*

Failing to adhere to a ceremony or a feast can't cause somebody to be accused of anything. However when the law says "don't do this" or "do that" and we fail to comply, then we *can* be found guilty! It is therefore clear to see that not only were the ceremonial aspects of the law cancelled, but also the entire penal side which stood *against* us!

Christ, the End of the Law

The truth is that for a believer the law has ended. Paul wrote how his heart yearned for the Israelites who still tried to live according to the law after Christ had died to set us free from it (and the same applies to us today):

> *Brethren, my heart's desire and prayer to God for Israel is that they may be saved. For I bear them witness that they have a zeal for God, but not according to knowledge. For they being ignorant of God's righteousness, and seeking to establish their own righteousness* [by still trying to live up to the requirements of the law], *have not submitted to the righteousness of God* [received by simply believing in Christ]. *For Christ is the end of the law for righteousness to everyone who believes* [we receive salvation and God's righteousness not by living under the law, but through believing in Christ!]. *(Rom 10:1-4 NKJV, annotations added)*

> *...that if you confess with your mouth the Lord Jesus and believe in your heart that God has raised Him from the dead, you will be saved. For with the heart one believes unto righteousness, and with the mouth confession is made unto salvation. (Rom 10:9-10 NKJV)*

Law →✝→ Grace

Super Abounding Grace!

Moreover the Law entered that the offense might abound. But where sin abounded, grace abounded much more. (Rom 5:20 NKJV)

This verse isn't referring to a particular sin, because if it did we'd never be able to tell exactly which sin Paul was referring to. Instead it refers to the inherent tendency to sin and hostility towards God that entered the human heart in the Garden of Eden. Through his disobedience Adam was turned into a sinner by nature. Adam then passed this inherent sinful nature on to all his offspring. Yes it was only a single act of disobedience, but it opened his heart for the sinful condition to enter.

Every human being inherited this sinful nature from Adam and the reason why the law was given was to *stimulate our sinful nature* so that we become more aware of our sinful condition.

Nevertheless death reigned from Adam to Moses, even over those who had not sinned according to the likeness of the transgression of Adam, who is a type of Him who was to come. (Rom 5:14 NKJV)

Because of Adam's sin, the whole world became guilty. If anybody were to end up eternally separated from God, it would not technically have been because of their own sins, but because they inherited Adam's sinful nature at birth. In the same way, nobody will inherit eternal life because of their own goodness or level of obedience, but only because of their faith in Jesus' perfect obedience:

But the free gift is not like the offense. For if by the one man's offense many died, much more the grace of God and the gift by the grace of the one Man, Jesus Christ, abounded to many. (Rom 5:15 NKJV)

Because of Jesus' obedience, those who believe in Him are justified by faith. It almost seems unfair that a person would be eternally condemned for sins they didn't even commit, but likewise it's also unfair that people should go to heaven because none of us deserve it.

The Law Arouses Sin-Consciousness

When God gave the law, it was meant to come in beside sinners to show how huge our lack of holiness really was. It wasn't given to turn mankind into sinners, because sin and death already existed even before the law was given (Romans 5:14 above). The purpose of the law was to show mankind the depth of their depravity. God didn't introduce the law because He wanted to make us sin more - He wanted us to be more conscious of our sins and the fact that we had an utterly sinful nature. Notice in Romans 5:15 (above) that Paul does not say "offenses" (plural) but "offense" (singular), which is a reference to the sin or sinful state of Adam. A few of the heroes of the faith made the following comments:

Charles Spurgeon: "A stick is crooked, but you do not notice how crooked it is until you place a straight rule by the side of it. You have a handkerchief, and it seems to be quite white. You could hardly wish it to be whiter. But you lay it down on the newly fallen snow, and you wonder how you could ever have thought it to be white at all. So the pure and holy law of God, when our eyes are opened to see its purity, shows up our sin in its true blackness, and in that way it makes sin to abound. But this is for our good, for that sight of our sin awakens us to a sense of our true condition, leads us to repentance, drives us by faith to the precious blood of Jesus, and no longer permits us to rest in our self-righteousness. It was the practical result of the giving of the law that men became greater sinners than they were before, and it was the design of the law that they should see themselves to be greater sinners than before. The law is the looking-glass in which we see our spots, but it is not the basin in which we wash them away. The law has a provoking power, for such is the perversity of our (old) nature that, no sooner do we hear the command, "You shall not do so-and-so," than at once we want to do it".

Dave Guzik: "The flaws in a precious stone abound when contrasted with a perfect stone, or when put against a contrasting backdrop. God's perfect law exposes our flaws and makes our sin abound. There is another way that the law makes sin abound. Because of the sinfulness of my heart, when I see a line drawn I want to cross over it. In this sense, the law makes sin abound because it draws many clear lines between right and wrong that my sinful heart wants to break. Therefore, the law makes me sin more – but not because there is anything wrong in the law, only because there is something deeply wrong in the human condition".

John Piper: "I take it to mean that one crucial function of the law is to turn our original sin into actual transgressions of specific commandments. First, we are guilty in Adam and sinful by nature and then the law confronts us with the specific will of God: "Don't steal. Don't lie. Don't covet." And the effect is that it turns sinful nature into specific sinful acts of transgression. One writer said it well: the law makes little Adams out of us all". ("The law has the function of turning those it addresses into 'their own Adam.")

So we see the law was given so that sin might abound. Our key verse however says that where sin abounded, grace abounded much more! Let's look at some quotes on grace that abounds:

Wayne Barber: "Now there are two words used in that verse for abound or increase. The first one is *pleonazo* (used with "sin"), which means "is more than enough" or "to have enough." The other word (used with grace), *perisseuo*, is actually a synonym, but when they are used together, they are saying different things. *Pleonazo* means to abound, but *perisseuo* means to go even beyond that (and) takes it to a greater extreme. Not only that, but Paul put a preposition, *huper*, in front of the word *perisseuo* (*huperperisseuo*). So what he is saying is that not only does grace extend beyond where sin increased, but grace goes WAY beyond".

In his book, "What's So Amazing About Grace," Phillip Yancey points out that part of our problem is in the nature of grace itself. "Grace is scandalous. It's hard to accept, hard to believe, and hard to receive. Grace shocks us in what it offers. It is truly not of this world. It frightens us with what it does for sinners. Grace teaches us that God does for others what we would never do for them. We would save the "not-so-bad". God starts with prostitutes and then works downward from there. Grace is a gift that costs everything to the giver and nothing to the receiver. It is given to those who don't deserve it, barely recognize it, and hardly appreciate it. That's why God alone gets the glory in your salvation. Jesus did all the work when he died on the cross".

The law added transgressions, showing even more clearly the super-abounding (*huperperisseuo*) grace of God. Grace did not set aside the law, but rather completely satisfied it. As deep as sin goes, God's grace goes deeper. As wide as sin is, God's grace is wider. When sin abounded, grace super-abounded. God's grace is greater than all our sin.

Barnhouse also comments on Paul's use of "abounds" and "super-abounds": "In the Greek, these are two different words. "Where sin overflowed, grace flooded in." Where sin measurably increased, grace immeasurably increased. Where sin abounded - *pleonazo* - grace did much more abound - *huper-perisseuo*. The prefix *huper* is like the Latin "super". The movie ads have taught us what "super" does to a word. Instead of being colossal, something is super-colossal. So, where sin could be measured by multiplying the number of commands of the law by the number of human beings in the world, grace could never be measured because it would require the multiplication of the number of acts of God's grace by the infinity of His being. Our text might well read: "Where sin was finite, grace was infinite."

Why is it so easy for people to believe that they were condemned and made sinners because of someone else's sin, but they find it so hard to believe that similarly, by someone else's superior, perfect and all encompassing sacrifice, they were made righteous forever?

Law →✝→ Grace

The Importance of Our Thoughts

(Andrew Wommack was a great inspiration for this chapter - his free audio series on Christian Philosophy¹ is highly recommended).

Psychology today and through the past few centuries (through propaganda and the media) has found its way right into our modern day way of thinking and is responsible for many misconceptions regarding human emotions and the way we interpret them.

Psychology tells us that we are only victims of our circumstances and they put the chain of events in the following order, where the one impacts the one next in line to it:

Circumstances ▶ Emotions ▶ Thoughts ▶ Deeds

In other words, we are just victims of our circumstances. If the above pattern is true, it implies that when things aren't going well our emotions will be troubled, which will lead to thoughts of anxiety, depression and stress, which can then lead to addictive behavioral patterns like eating disorders, pornography, alcoholism, a bad self image and even suicide in some cases, because these emotions eventually have to be vented in some form or another!

This is also the reason why millions of people across the world who struggle with bad habits and sin say: "I was created this way. I can't help it, I was born like this". Although it is true that we are born into this world with Adam's fallen nature, it still requires active choices on our part to cultivate bad habits. An alcoholic for example has to *choose* to raise the bottle to his lips every time; the bottle doesn't get there by itself.

People also tend to think that they will not be held accountable for their thoughts. However just like our deeds, we *can* control our thoughts (yes we can!) and make them obedient to Christ. Destructive patterns of sin and perversion in people's lives are simply the result of those people embracing, indulging and persisting in lustful and self gratifying thoughts year after year. They often wonder why they feel so regularly "tempted" by the devil, while in fact the devil is only standing on the sidelines, watching them destroy their own lives!

Think about this: When it comes to sin, we can rarely go anywhere and do anything in our physical body if we have not been there in our mind first.

This message is not meant to condemn. It is simply a key to help us see the importance of the role that our thoughts play in the process of our lives and to help us understand how we are influenced by it. We are also aiming to expose the lie of modern day psychology, namely that we are just victims of our circumstances. The Bible is very clear about this sort of thing, where clever philosophies try to exalt themselves above the truth of God's Word:

> *Beware lest anyone cheat you through philosophy and empty deceit, according to the tradition of men, according to the basic principles of the world, and not according to Christ. (Col 2:8 NKJV)*

The aforementioned psychological pattern is definitely not in line with the Word of God, which tells us that things are actually lined up as follows:

Thoughts ▶ Emotions ▶ Deeds ▶ Circumstances

Everything begins with our thoughts.

> *And do not be conformed to this world, but be transformed by the renewing of your mind, that you may prove what is that good and acceptable and perfect will of God. (Rom 12:2 NKJV)*

> *We demolish arguments and every pretension that sets itself up against the knowledge of God, and we take captive every thought to make it obedient to Christ. (2 Cor 10: 5 NKJV)*

King Solomon, one of the wisest men to ever walk the earth, wrote the following:

> *For as he thinks in his heart, so is he. (Prov 23:7a NKJV)*

We are victims of our mindsets, whether it's good or bad. If we indulge in self pity, defeat, depravity and malice our lives will be a testimony of this and we will simply learn to accept whatever our circumstances or the devil throw at us.

However when our thoughts are full of what God says we are, when we meditate upon His Word, on His goodness, His grace towards us and His promises, our emotions will begin to change. We will see that we are fellow heirs with Christ

(Ephesians 3:6) and partakers of the glory of God (1 Peter 5:1), not created to keep begging for scraps from the table, but to live life in abundance! Our emotions will have a reaction on the things we do, since we are supernaturally inspired by truth, and as we start living a life of worship, a life that makes room for the presence of God, praising God continually for His goodness and provision and seeking first the Kingdom, our circumstances will supernaturally begin to change (Matthew 6:33).

Like Jesus, we can command storms to be still, sickness to vanish and any gloomy circumstances to line up with the truth of God's Word, namely that we are His children; that we are blessed beyond any curse; that Christ carried our punishment for us and that no condemnation has the right to come our way!

It all begins with this: *What are our thoughts occupied with?* We are required to be faithful stewards of our thoughts, just as much as with the things we do.

"The devil wants to rob you of your peace because agitated people rarely hear the voice of God. In a time of opportunity, the word is "distraction" on the devil's agenda, whereas God's agenda is laser like focus – I was born and raised for this time!" - Rob Rufus (City Church International, Hong Kong).

Let us not be robbed of our destiny, which is a life full of the glory of our King! Let's set our minds on the things of God and most of all, on our Father Himself!

> *If then you were raised with Christ, seek those things which are above, where Christ is, sitting at the right hand of God. Set your mind on things above, not on things on the earth. For you died, and your life is hidden with Christ in God. (Col 3:1-3)*

Law →✝→ Grace

Saved by Grace, But What Comes Next?

When we talk about grace, most people will say they know grace and that they have been saved by grace through faith:

> *For by grace you have been saved through faith, and that not of yourselves; it is the gift of God, not of works, lest anyone should boast. (Eph 2:8-9)*

But the majority will then add that these verses only refer to the actual point of salvation. From this point we need to move on to the more important aspects of the Christian life like sanctification, living a "holy" lifestyle and becoming more effective for God. They say we have to "work out" our own salvation, completely misquoting Philippians 2:12. This verse doesn't say we need to "work for" our salvation. "Working out" our salvation means to "figure out" (i.e. "work out") how beautiful, complete and wonderful our salvation is. It also means to start allowing what's on the inside of us flow outward. The Holy Spirit wants to touch the outside world from within us. That's what it means to "work out" our salvation.

The churches of the Galatians started well. They knew they were saved by grace initially, but then they started relying on their own efforts to "keep" themselves saved. Let's see what Paul wrote to them:

> *O foolish Galatians! Who has bewitched you that you should not obey the truth, before whose eyes Jesus Christ was clearly portrayed among you as crucified? This only I want to learn from you: Did you receive the Spirit by the works of the law, or by the hearing of faith? Are you so foolish? Having begun in the Spirit, are you now being made perfect by the flesh? (Gal 3:1-3 NKJV)*

When Paul talked about grace to the Galatians, he wasn't talking about being born again to non believers; he was talking to believers, people that were *already* born again. He said that they had started well in grace, but now they had come under the pressure of people that preached law, who said they had to be perfectly obedient in order to receive God's blessings. Here in Galatians 3 Paul was telling them that they should *continue* in the grace of God, just like he told the church of the Colossians:

> Col 2:6 *As you therefore have received Christ Jesus the Lord* [by simply believing and not by trying to earn it], *so walk in Him. (Col 2:6 NKJV, annotations and emphasis added)*

Now think for a moment; how did we receive Him? We simply believed. How should we therefore continue to walk in Him now that we are born again? By simply believing. If grace was enough to save us, grace is enough to keep us.

God's blessings, healing and prosperity does not come through striving, through our own works of righteousness or through trying to live holy. It comes through being established in the gift of righteousness, the righteousness we first received as a gift when we came into Christ. We can never leave our foundation behind. The bigger we build the building, the more we have to strengthen the foundation, which is grace.

Sanctification?

In the modern day church there is a dangerous misconception that God initially accepts a person unconditionally on the basis of grace, but once they are saved they now suddenly have to perform at a certain level for God to continue to accept and bless them. The Bible talks about two types of righteousness: The righteousness of God (receiving salvation, God's approval and blessings by faith) and self righteousness (going back under the law and trying to receive all the above by trying to earn them through good works). But prevailing in most churches today is a third type of righteousness, one that is mentioned nowhere in the Bible: Once we are saved, we leave behind grace and the righteousness of God as a gift and try to become more righteous by our own good works - this teaching is often disguised behind another misunderstood word called "sanctification", which by the way has nothing to do with trying to sin less.

The only way to get free from this trap is by becoming more established in the righteousness of God as a gift. Once we realize that we can never add to the righteousness that was given to us as a gift and that our best efforts are like dirty rags, we will see that only by trusting in the perfect obedience of the One Man, Jesus Christ, can we have confidence before God.

> *But we are all like an unclean thing, And all our righteousnesses are like filthy rags. (Isa 64:6 NKJV)*

This verse says says all our <u>RIGHT</u>eousnesses are like filthy rags, not our <u>UN</u>righteousnesses. So it is not talking about our mistakes, but about our good works. Good works done from a motive of trying to earn God's love through them are considered to be like filthy rags. The original Hebrew language actually refers to a woman's menstrual cloth - that's really how bad it is!

Some preachers start well, preaching grace and unconditional love to get people saved. But then when they see people's lives change because of the grace of God, they start seeing this as a fruit of their own teaching and they begin to emphasize holy living at the cost of grace.

Take the Test

How do we know that we have been established in the grace of God? If we can say immediately after we have stumbled morally that we are the righteousness of God in Christ Jesus (2 Corinthians 5:21) and that nothing we ever do can change that! Remember we're not saying that people should use grace as an excuse to sin (see the chapter entitled "IS GRACE SIMPLY A LICENSE TO SIN?").

We need the innocence of a child restored to us, feeling as though we have never sinned because God has forgiven all our sins past present and future:

> *Their sins and their lawless deeds I will remember no more. (Heb 10:17 NKJV)*

When we reach that place of boldly approaching the throne of grace with our conscience clean of any accusations from Satan, we can say we have been established in the gift of righteousness. God doesn't want us to feel guilty about any sins, because why should we be reminded of our mistakes if God doesn't remember them anymore?

> *Therefore, brethren, having boldness to enter the Holiest by the blood of Jesus, by a new and living way which He consecrated for us, through the veil, that is, His flesh, and having a High Priest over the house of God, let us draw near with a true heart in full assurance of faith, having our hearts sprinkled from an evil conscience and our bodies washed with pure water. (Heb 10:19-22 NKJV)*

Law →✝→ Grace

Do Christians Need to Confess Their Sins?
Pt 1 (James 5:16)

Just the pure mention of somebody questioning a topic like this could offend and anger a lot of people.

Confessing is different from repenting: repentance has to do with a person changing their thinking, while confession means to bring into remembrance something from their past. We've already dealt with repentance earlier. Let's now look at *confessing*.

The real question that we should ask when talking about confessing our sins is this: "When a Christian sins (makes a mistake), is their right standing with God lost and can that right standing only be restored if the person confesses the sin?" If we can forget for a few minutes all the things we've heard people say, including the traditions of men that have been passed down to us, as well as the way we "think" we should react when we make a mistake, then let's see what the Word says.

There are only two verses in the New Covenant (1 John 1:9 and James 5:16) that deal with confessing sin and both are mostly misunderstood. Firstly we will look at James 5:16 and in the next chapter at 1 John 1:9.

> *Confess your trespasses to one another, and pray for one another, that you may be healed. The effective fervent prayer of a righteous man avails much. (Jam 5:16 NKJV)*

There are no verses in the *New Covenant* (after the cross) other than James 5:16 that tell *believing Holy Spirit filled Christians* to confess their sins or trespasses. Furthermore this verse does not instruct us to confess to God. James 5:16 says we have to confess our faults to each other - *not to God*.

Now some scholars have interpreted James 5:14-16 to mean that God makes people sick because they have sin in their life. These same verses have also been misinterpreted to mean that people have to confess their sins to priests or to the elders of a church and that they will subsequently be forgiven their sins and healed if they confess to a person. Let's read the two verses preceding our key verse:

> *Is anyone among you sick? Let him call for the elders of the church, and let them pray over him, anointing him with oil in the name of the Lord. And the prayer of faith will save the sick, and the Lord will raise him up. And if he has committed sins, he will be forgiven. (Jam 5:14-16 NKJV)*

After the cross God has forgiven *all* our sins past, present & future (Hebrews 10:17, Colossians 3:13). The only transgressions that we as New Covenant believers may still need forgiveness for, is *from* the people we have sinned against. However God has already forgiven us for these sins as well. Since none of us are perfect in all we do, we sometimes offend, hurt or harm people. And since people are not as gracious and merciful as God, we need to make amends with them. And that's where James 5:16 comes in: *"Confess your trespasses to one another, and pray for one another, that you may be healed…"*

Our right standing with God does not change, but our relationships with others *can* be damaged and need to be restored. When we humbly confess to those we have wronged (and if they will receive us in humility) it opens the door for that restoration to happen.

The Vertical and Horizontal Dimensions

There are two relational dimensions to always keep in mind: Firstly there is the *vertical* dimension pertaining to our relationship with God. The foundation for this relationship is the finished work of the cross and God's love for us. It's *not* based on our unstable level of obedience.

Secondly there is the *horizontal* dimension pertaining to our relationships with other people. These relationships are definitely based on our own levels of loyalty, love, affection and good works. By this we are *not* implying that people should give their best to other people and just present God with their second hand scraps. However the basis of God's love for us is not grounded in our level of good works or obedience, but in *who* we are: His beloved children who have the Holy Spirit living on the inside of us!

Even when David had called for a ballot (census) of Israel, God gave him the option of choosing one of three punishments for doing such a thing (under the law God had to punish man but under grace Jesus bore the punishment for our sins). But because David knew God's true nature, he chose to be punished by God, and not by man:

> *So Gad* [the prophet] *came to David and said to him, "Thus says the LORD: 'Choose for yourself, either three years of famine, or three months to be defeated by your foes with the sword of your enemies overtaking you, or else for three days the sword of the LORD - the plague in the land, with the angel of the LORD destroying throughout all the territory of Israel.' Now consider what answer I should take back to Him who sent me." And David said to Gad, "I am in great distress. Please let me fall into the hand of the LORD, for His mercies are very great; but do not let me fall into the hand of man".* (1 Chron 21:11-13, annotations added)

We are always safe and secure in God's unconditional love, but the love of people is dependent upon our own good behavior. We will find that very few people will continue to love us if we persist in insincerity, lying, fits of rage, violent behavior, etc.

To clinch this and prove that the context of James 5:16 is about our relationships with *other people* and not about confessing our sins to God, let's read a few more verses from James 5, just a few verses prior to our key verse:

> *Indeed the wages of the laborers who mowed your fields, which you kept back by fraud, cry out; and the cries of the reapers have reached the ears of the Lord of Hosts. (Jam 5:4 NKJV)*

> *Do not grumble against one another, brethren, lest you be condemned... (Jam 5:9 NKJV)*

In this context, where people have wronged and hurt each other, James is telling them to make amends; to be reconciled with each other and to confess their faults to each other, especially at beds of affliction where death and eternity seem to be near approaching.

Another interpretation is that James 5:16 does *not* mean that we should reveal our sins and trespasses to every second person. James implies that we should confide our problems to a close, trusted friend so that he or she can help us by praying to God for help in overcoming it.

Law →✝→ Grace

Do Christians Need to Confess Their Sins? Pt 2 (1 John 1:9)

In Part 1 we spoke about James 5:16 and the fact that it relates to our relationships with other people. Now we'll look at the only other verse in the New Covenant which talks about confessing our sins: 1 John 1:9.

Firstly and most importantly note we are *not* propagating a sinful lifestyle. We are *not* encouraging people to just go out and commit hideous deeds of licentiousness and immorality. We believe in obeying God and living a holy lifestyle, but these are only the fruit. The root is being established in grace and righteousness and knowing who we are in Christ.

> *If we confess our sins, He is faithful and just to forgive us our sins, and to cleanse us from all unrighteousness. (1 John 1:9 NKJV)*

This verse has to be read in the context of the rest of the book of John - written to a group of believers whose ranks had previously been infiltrated by teachers of Gnosticism[1]. The apostle John seems to be gentle whenever he addresses the Christians, calling them "my little children". But in other parts of his letter, when he is countering the teachings of the Gnostics, he becomes quite protective of his brothers and sisters in Christ and his words quite harsh.

At the time that John wrote this letter, the Gnostics had *already left* the Christians:

> *They went out from us, but they were not of us; for if they had been of us, they would no doubt have continued with us: but they went*

> *out, that they might be made manifest that they were not all of us.*
> *1 John 2:19 NKJV)*

However remnants of the Gnosticism teachings were still confusing the Christians that remained.

Gnostics are people who believe that creation is flawed and that it was fashioned by a flawed creator, a movement out of which the "Church of Jesus Christ of the Latter Day Saints" (Mormons) has arisen. The *gnōsis* referred to in the term is a form of mystic, exposed but also obscure knowledge through which the spiritual elements of humanity are reminded of their true origins within the superior Godhead, being thus permitted to escape materiality (or by implication to enter eternity). Consequently, within the sects of Gnosticism only the "pneumatics" or "psychics" (the two highest forms of spirituality) obtain *gnōsis*.

The duty of (spiritual) man is to escape the material world by the aid of the hidden knowledge (gnosis). Jesus of Nazareth is identified by some Gnostic sects as an embodiment of the Supreme Being who became incarnate to bring *gnosis* to the earth. In other Gnostic sects (e.g. the Notzrim and Mandaeans) he is considered a false messiah who perverted the teachings entrusted to him by John the Baptist. They also believe that there is no such thing as sin in the world *and as an unbeliever that you do not have to acknowledge that you are a sinner to be born again.*

Even though the books of 1 to 3 John were addressed to the church, 1 John 1:9 was *not* a command for people to grovel in sack cloth and ash. Instead it is simply a statement to contradict the false teachings of the Gnostics.

There were people in the Apostle John's church (who had not yet been born again) who were self righteously claiming that they did not need to confess their sins to receive eternal life, or that they did not have any sins! They were still confused by the teachings of the Gnostics, even though the Gnostics had already left. John countered their lies with the following:

> *If we say that we have no sin, we deceive ourselves, and the truth*
> *is not in us. (1 John 1:8 NKJV)*

And then in the next verse he reveals how to be saved:

> *If we confess our sins, He is faithful and just to forgive us our sins,*
> *and to cleanse us from <u>all unrighteousness</u>. (1 John 1:9 NKJV,*
> *emphasis added)*

God would cleanse them from *all* unrighteousness if they would only confess that they needed to be forgiven of their sins.

Paul Ellis (Escape To Reality)[2] puts it as follows: *"How do I know that John is talking to unbelievers and not Christians? Because he is addressing people who are walking in darkness (v.6), who need to be purified from all unrighteousness (v.9) and who, by insisting that they have never sinned, are making God out to be a liar (v.10).*

What message does John have for sinners who don't think they're sinners? "Acknowledge your sinful state, turn to God and receive His gift of forgiveness." There's only one thing that stops a sinner from receiving God's grace and that's unbelief. If you don't see your need for forgiveness, you are well and truly lost. You may claim to know God but He doesn't know you."

If 1 John 1:9 were addressed to the believing Christians (the ones who were already saved), it would then contradict the following verse:

> *Little children, I write to you because you <u>have been forgiven</u> your sins through His name. (1 John 2:12 NKJV, emphasis added)*

Why would John command people to confess their sins if he says a few verses later that they *have already been* forgiven? Also, if confessing our sins to God were such an important practice in the life of a believer, why did the writer of the majority of the New Testament, Paul the Apostle, not command us to do it even once?

Under the New Covenant *all* our sins (past, present and future) have been forgiven. Now we don't need to forgive others anymore in order for God to forgive us; now we forgive others because we *have already been* forgiven.

> *...even as Christ <u>forgave</u> you, so you also must do. (Col 3:13b NKJV, emphasis added)*

The born again spirit of a Christian is 100% righteous and will remain 100% righteous for all of eternity in despite their less than perfect behavior during their remaining time on the earth. If this were not the case, there would be no other way to explain the following "contradicting" verses:

> [8] *If we say that we have no sin, we deceive ourselves, and the truth is not in us.* [9] *If we confess our sins, He is faithful and just to forgive us our sins and to cleanse us from all unrighteousness.* [10] *If we say that we have not sinned, we make Him a liar, and His word is not in us. (1 John 1:8-10, NKJV)*

Now compare these three verses against the following "seemingly" conflicting verse:

> *Whoever has been born of God does not sin, for His seed remains in him; and he cannot sin, because he has been born of God. (1 John 3:9 NKJV)*

The only explanation is that in the first three verses, even though John used the word "we", he was in fact not referring to believers, but in an inclusive manner, to unbelievers. As a shepherd and a preacher he was identifying with the lost in an open display of God's love, saying "*We* have all sinned, *we* all need to repent". Instead of attacking and ridiculing the unbelievers openly, he was tactfully saying something along the lines of this (compare these with the verses above):

(v8) If any person claims to be without sin, they are deceived and the truth (Christ) does not live inside them (because Christ said "I am the truth, the way and the life). (v9) But if such a person (a sinner) acknowledges they are sinful and in need of a Savior, God who is faithful will forgive them *all* of their sins and wash them clean of *all* unrighteousness (implying that they are now clean for ever). (v10) However if any person claims they have never sinned, they make God into a liar and willingly reject the truth of His word.

Think about it this way: What does a person have to do to be born again? They have to admit that they need a Savior and put their faith in Christ (Romans 10:9-10). Therefore if any person claims to be without sin *before* putting their faith in Christ, they are deceived and blinded to the truth. This is the heresy that John was countering in this epistle.

Countless doctrines have been formulated by the modern day church about confessing our sins to God, all based on this one verse (1 John 1:9). It's quite amazing if we realize there are no other verses in the entire New Covenant that back up this theory! It's even more remarkable when we realize that this verse was not even intended for Christians who have put their trust in the grace of God, but for self righteous people!

Rob Rufus (City Church International, Hong Kong)[3] said the following:

"There are millions of people who have turned their backs on Jesus and have left the church not because they are intentionally evil or sinful people, but because they are sincere people that for years and years have been taught a mixture of Old Covenant Law and New Covenant grace. These people eventually came to a place where they felt that other Christians and they themselves were such hypocrites and that their failures and mistakes were so great, that their discouragement drove them away from Jesus into the wilderness. They gave up on Jesus and His Word, although they still love Him in their hearts."

Being "Real" With God

But now the question might arise: "Why would God *not* want us to confess our sins to Him? After all, we do make mistakes!" The answer is simple: Because walking around the whole day remembering all the bad things we have done will not bring us closer to God! Jesus already paid the full price so that we could have unbroken fellowship with the Father. This means that when we make a mistake, it does not break our fellowship or right standing with God. Jesus was forsaken by his Father on the cross so that we would never have to experience that!

Some may argue: "But I want to be *genuine* with God and talk to Him about all my mistakes." Well if people believe they need to be "genuine" with God about their mistakes, then to be *really* genuine they should rather act in faith, because without faith it is impossible to please God (Hebrews 11:6). How much faith does it take to look at our mistakes and feel miserable about them? None. On the other hand, it takes faith to believe we are forgiven, loved, holy, perfect and righteous, even after we have just messed up.

We shouldn't be surprised at the puzzled look on God's face whenever we try to confess our sins to Him. This is because He doesn't actually know what we're talking about. After all, He promised to never remember our sins ever again (Isaiah 43:25).

Be Conscious of Your Righteousness!

Does this mean that we can just go out and live a life of full blown wickedness and depravity because our fellowship with God will never be broken, even if we sin? No! But it definitely means that God wants us to have confidence before Him and to be more aware of our righteousness and His grace than of our shortcomings and mistakes.

> *Having therefore, brethren, boldness to enter into the holiest by the blood of Jesus, By a new and living way, which he hath consecrated for us, through the veil, that is to say, his flesh; And having an high priest over the house of God; Let us draw near with a true heart in full assurance of faith, having our hearts sprinkled from an evil conscience, and our bodies washed with pure water. (Heb 10:19-22 NKJV)*

How can we have boldness before God if we have to grovel on our knees and plead for the forgiveness of our sins every time we pray? And if we can't have confidence before God, how then can we even dream to stand in front of a blind person and say confidently: "Blind eyes open in the name of Jesus!" We'd always feel that God does not want to use us because we have too much sin in our lives.

No amount of crying, confessing, remembering our sins, emotional torment or anything we can do can add to the finished work of the cross, where our sins were forgiven once and for all!

So whenever we find ourselves conscious of our sins, we simply say: "Thank You Jesus for the perfect work of the cross that has removed my sins completely. Thank you Holy Spirit for convicting me of righteousness; not my own, but the righteousness given to me as a gift! I praise You that nothing that I do can ever change that or ever separate me from Your love!"

Tony Ide (Freedom Life Fellowship, Perth, Australia)[4] says that *"grace does not mean the denial of occasional mistakes in our lives - that is a dangerous thing to do - rather grace removes the punishment and guilt of that sin. Grace is what makes us worthy!"*

Rob Rufus presented the following brilliant argument: *"Let's pretend for a moment that Christians do have to confess their sins to God, then for the sake of integrity these people should remain consistent. They should not only confess those sins which they think are the big sins, but also all the little sins. Romans 14:23 says that anything a Christian doesn't do out of faith is sin.*

This means that we have to monitor every single little thing we do the entire day and if we find ourselves doing anything without faith (eat, go to work, go to church, drive home, talk to our children, take off our shoes, worry about anything, etc.) then that is sin and we should stop whatever we are doing at that moment and confess that we have sinned, because God has now cut Himself off from us and our right standing with Him has been broken and we stand in danger of being thrown into hellfire for sinning."

Is God Schizophrenic?

Does God sit in heaven with a pencil and eraser, monitoring our every move the entire day? Does He blot out our names from the Book of Life every time we mess up, just to write it back in when we confess? What about if we forget to confess? Is our salvation really *that* insecure? Does God change His mind *that* easily?

To Confess or Not to Confess?

In closing, the Bible teaches all unbelievers to confess their sins to God to be born again and come into Christ (1 John 1:9), but the Bible does not teach born again Christians to confess their sins to God.

There is however nothing wrong with confiding in our loving Father about our struggles. He understands us better than anybody else. But it's all about our motives. When we mess up, do we run to Him feeling guilty and condemned like a murderer about to be condemned to retribution? Or do we ask Him for wisdom in overcoming the habits of our unrenewed minds, knowing we stand completely forgiven and holy in His sight?

Law →✝→ Grace

The Purpose of the New Covenant

The main purpose of the New Covenant was not primarily for God to come and change our external behavior; the primary purpose was that God changed the way He related to mankind, namely through grace, resulting in an spontaneous change in behavior due to mankind receiving revelation about God's vast and infinite love for them.

Under the Old Covenant God dealt with people on the basis of their external behavior, namely their level of obedience to the law. Under this system God left people to their own devices and judged them according to their works. People were punished and cursed when they broke the law. But then came the New Covenant and God dealt with the internal problem, namely people's fallen sinful nature. Those who put their faith in Him were changed from the inside; God bestowing them with the very nature of his Son, Jesus Christ. He also credited the perfect obedience of Jesus to their account.

The believer's old sinful nature has been crucified with Christ and their spirit made 100% righteous:

> ...*knowing this, that our old man was crucified with Him, that the body of sin might be done away with, that we should no longer be slaves of sin. For he who has died has been freed from sin. (Rom 6:6-7 NKJV)*

This is the way He now sees believers: blameless and fully righteous in His sight:

> *And you, who once were alienated and enemies in your mind by wicked works, yet now He has reconciled in the body of His flesh through death, to present you holy, and blameless, and above reproach in His sight. (Col 1:21-22 NKJV)*

Before we were born again, we were enemies of God and we were alienated from Him in two ways:

1. We had a sinful nature inside us and we were slaves to this sinful nature, running after every evil thing that gratified its desires:

   ...among whom also we all once conducted ourselves in the lusts of our flesh, fulfilling the desires of the flesh and of the mind, and were by nature children of wrath, just as the others. (Eph 2:3 NKJV)

   We were alive to sin because of our sinful nature, and dead towards God.

2. We were also under the law, which utterly condemned us and showed us how sinful we were:

   Now we know that whatever the law says, it says to those who are under the law, that every mouth may be stopped, and all the world may become guilty before God. Therefore by the deeds of the law no flesh will be justified in His sight, for by the law is the knowledge of sin. (Rom 3:19-20 NKJV)

But Romans 6:6-7 (above) says that we have now become dead to sin. We've become the friends of God and we were also united with Him in two ways:

1. Our sinful nature was crucified with Christ and our spirit made alive towards God; in other words: we were born again. The perfect righteousness of Jesus Christ was imputed to us and all the benefits and blessings of His obedience have been credited to us because of our faith in Him:

   Therefore as by the offense of one, judgment came upon all men to condemnation; even so by the righteousness of one, the free gift came upon all men unto justification of life (Rom 5:18 KJV).

2. The law has been nullified, nailed to the cross with Jesus:

   ...having wiped out the handwriting of requirements that was against us, which was contrary to us. And He has taken it out of the way, having nailed it to the cross. (Col 2:14 NKJV)

God now relates to believers on the basis of the obedience of Jesus Christ. God does not attribute their sins to them, but instead delights in them with the love and passion of a proud Father. Now God doesn't just see us as if we've never sinned - He sees us as if we have perfectly obeyed all the laws our entire life!

But how can all of this be true when none of us could ever deserve to be given a gift like this? That's exactly it: *Nobody deserves grace.* It is a free gift from God, given to those who believe in Him. If we were ever able to earn it, it wouldn't be called a "gift" anymore, would it?

> *For by grace you have been saved through faith, and that not of yourselves; it is the gift of God. (Eph 2:8 NKJV, emphasis added)*

Law →✝→ Grace

Making Your Brother Stumble

Looking back, it's easy for us to sometimes laugh about the beliefs we had when we first became Christians. Some of us still get uncomfortable when someone asks us what our star sign is, or the way we hurriedly skip over the horoscopes in the paper. But sometimes on the road to maturity, we may presume to know too much.

The Corinthians were proud about how much they knew. In 1 Corinthians 8:1 when Paul begins to talk to them about eating food that has been sacrificed to idols, he says "We all have knowledge." Now previously they had written Paul a letter, enquiring of him in an almost rhetorical fashion about this matter of eating food that has been sacrificed to idols. They knew that idols were nothing and that there is only one true God. And since Jesus declared *all* food to be clean, they knew that they could eat anything they wanted to, whether it had been sacrificed to idols or not:

> *"There is nothing that enters a man from outside which can defile him; but the things which come out of him, those are the things that defile a man." (Mark 7:15 NKJV)*

So being proud of the fact that they knew so much, basically they only expected Paul to confirm their point of view. However, Paul saw right through their pride and pointed out to them that they had become puffed up in their knowledge:

> *Now concerning things offered to idols: We know that we all have knowledge. Knowledge puffs up, but love edifies. (1 Cor 8:1 NKJV)*

In 1 Corinthians 8:7 Paul continues to explain what he meant by this. The Corinthians, having become puffed up by their knowledge, had neglected to love those around them that were not as strong in the faith as they were. Some Christians who were still immature in the faith did not yet have the revelation that nothing in itself is unclean. Christ through the cross had made everything clean and He removed *all* curses from us, whether those curses could come to us through food, through ornaments or objects brought into our homes. He took onto Himself all curses or spells that could be cast onto us by witches, Satanists, fortune tellers and wizards; all the curses that could come onto us through disobedience, by eating unclean food, breaking the 10 Commandments or anything else!

> *Christ has redeemed us from the curse of the law, having become a curse for us (for it is written, "Cursed is everyone who hangs on a tree"). (Gal 3:13 NKJV)*

Paul points the Corinthians to something very important at the end of 1 Corinthians 8:1: "...but love edifies." Paul had written the Christians in Rome the same thing previously:

> *I know and am convinced by the Lord Jesus that there is nothing unclean of itself; but to him who considers anything to be unclean, to him it is unclean. Yet if your brother is grieved because of your food, you are no longer walking in love. Do not destroy with your food the one for whom Christ died. (Rom 14:14-15 NKJV)*

Not Just Food...

Now this matter of food can be applied to just about anything and it simply comes down to us not being the cause of stumbling to those who are not yet strong in the faith.

> *But beware lest somehow this liberty of yours become a stumbling block to those who are weak. (1 Cor 8:9 NKJV)*

Paul was saying that we should not let our freedom in eating certain foods, drinking certain drinks, watching certain movies, going to certain places, etc. be the cause of stumbling and offense to someone that has not yet reached that place of maturity and freedom in Christ.

In verse 7 and 10 Paul asks the Corinthians what it would mean for a Christian that has less knowledge, to see someone that they respect, eating the food that has been offered to an idol:

> *However, there is not in everyone that knowledge; for some, with consciousness of the idol, until now eat it as a thing offered to an idol; and their conscience, being weak, is defiled. (1 Cor 8:7 NKJV)*

> *For if anyone sees you who have knowledge eating in an idol's*
> *temple, will not the conscience of him who is weak be emboldened*
> *to eat those things offered to idols? (1 Cor 8:10 NKJV)*

The new and "weak" Christian might have just come out from under serving other gods and might still be thinking those gods are real and powerful. Now when they see the mature Christian eating that food, would it not suggest to the new Christian that those old beliefs might still have some truth in them?

The same applies to us. If a person that has just come out of a bad addiction to alcohol now sees us drink something a little stronger than milk (which by the way there is nothing wrong with), wouldn't that perhaps be a cause of stumbling to them?

In 1 Corinthians 10 Paul reinforced this again:

> *Let no one seek his own, but each one the other's well-being.*
> *Eat whatever is sold in the meat market, asking no questions for*
> *conscience' sake; for "the earth is the LORD's, and all its fullness."*
> *If any of those who do not believe invites you to dinner, and you*
> *desire to go, eat whatever is set before you, asking no question for*
> *conscience' sake. But if anyone says to you, "This was offered to*
> *idols," do not eat it for the sake of the one who told you, and for*
> *conscience' sake; for "the earth is the LORD's, and all its fullness."*
> *"Conscience," I say, not your own, but that of the other* [we should
> not eat it for the sake of the other person's conscience]. *For why*
> *is my liberty judged by another man's conscience? But if I partake*
> *with thanks, why am I evil spoken of for the food over which I give*
> *thanks? Therefore, whether you eat or drink, or whatever you do,*
> *do all to the glory of God. Give no offense, either to the Jews or to*
> *the Greeks or to the church of God, just as I also please all men in*
> *all things, not seeking my own profit, but the profit of many, that*
> *they may be saved. (1 Cor 10:24-33 NKJV, annotations added)*

Legalists Not to Take Advantage

On the contrary this does not give legalistic, self righteous people an excuse to put pressure on others (who are more free in the faith than they are) to stop doing this or that thing. If a mature Christian believes strongly with full integrity that things like dancing, drinking beer, smoking, watching violent movies, etc. is wrong, then there is nothing wrong with that. But a person should not make others believe that he / she is still weak in the faith and expect others to quit going to parties for their sake. Such a person should rather reflect on their beliefs and convictions and question whether the freedom that was purchased on the cross is perhaps much bigger and wider that they think. God dealt with the "sin problem" completely by punishing our sins fully on Jesus.

To conclude, if we are ever in doubt about whether we should do something or not, the following verses carry tremendous truth:

> *All things are lawful for me, but all things are not helpful. All things are lawful for me, but I will not be brought under the power of any. (1 Cor 6:12 NKJV)*

> *All things are lawful for me, but not all things are helpful; all things are lawful for me, but not all things edify. (1 Cor 10:23 NKJV)*

We have actually been given a legal license to indulge in just about anything, since our sins (even the future ones) have *all* been forgiven. We know however that not everything that entices our flesh is beneficial to us, such as chemical addictions, the praises of men, premarital sex, over-indulging in food, alcohol or even too much exercise. Although we have been freed from eternal and spiritual punishment of sin, sin carries its own destructive consequences here on the earth. We also know that if we've been truly born again, the desire of our born again spirit man is to live a life that pleases God and not indulge in these works of the flesh.

We've been given freedom to do whatever we want, which also includes making the right choices, loving one another, renewing our minds, healing the sick and advancing God's kingdom here on the earth!

> *For you, brethren, have been called to liberty; only do not use liberty as an opportunity for the flesh, but through love serve one another. (Gal 5:13 NKJV)*

Law →✝→ Grace

Sons of Abraham

The gospel of the New Covenant centers on the fact that God has changed the way He relates to mankind, not through the obedience of the law, but through grace alone. Through faith in Jesus Christ alone we are justified:

> *Knowing that a man is not justified by the works of the law, but by the faith of Jesus Christ, even we have believed in Jesus Christ, that we might be justified by the faith of Christ, and not by the works of the law: for by the works of the law shall no flesh be justified. (Gal 2:16 KJV)*

God made promises to Abraham in Genesis 12, saying that Abraham would be blessed, that God would make his name great and that *in* him all the nations of the earth would be blessed. God later in Genesis 15 and 17 confirmed these promises to Abraham with a covenant. And for the simple reason that *Abraham believed God*, God counted Abraham's faith to him as righteousness

> *And he believed in the LORD; and He accounted it to him for righteousness. (Gen 15:6 NKJV)*

God also blessed Abraham with an abundance of earthly possessions.

> *Abram was very rich in livestock, in silver, and in gold. (Gen 13:2 NKJV)*

Many years later, God made another covenant with a group of "stiff-necked" people. After having just brought them out of Egypt with ten mighty plagues and providing for their every need in the desert, Israel still refused to believe that God wanted to bless them *simply* because He is a good God. Now imagine for a second just *how hard* a person's heart needs to be for them to *still* believe that God isn't good after all He'd done for them! The writer of Hebrews tells us that this was the reason why Israel had to wander the desert for forty years before they could enter the Promised Land. All those who refused to believe in God's goodness died in the desert:

> *Beware, brethren, lest there be in any of you an evil heart of unbelief in departing from the living God. For who, having heard, rebelled? Indeed, was it not all who came out of Egypt, led by Moses? Now with whom was He angry forty years? Was it not with those who sinned, whose corpses fell in the wilderness? And to whom did He swear that they would not enter His rest, but to those who did not obey? So we see that they could not enter in because of unbelief. (Heb 3:12, 16-19 NKJV)*

And this is the reason why God gave them the law. Under the law they would have to live morally, perform rituals, make sacrifices and fully hold up their side of the deal in order for God to bless them. But through much of the Old Testament we see the sad unfolding of Israel's failure to comply with the requirements of the law. They were defeated, taken captive, their cities destroyed and they were scattered across the earth.

Two Covenants to Choose From

During the period starting from when the law was given, up to the cross, there existed two covenants in the earth: The covenant of the law and the covenant which God had made with Abraham. And here's the shocker: at any moment in their history, Israel could have chosen to come out from under the law and live again under the covenant that God had made with Abraham, once again believing that God would bless them and see them as righteous *not* because they tried to live up to the law, but simply because they believed in God. The covenant of the law did *not* cancel the promises that God made to Abraham!

> *Now to Abraham and his Seed were the promises made. He does not say, "And to seeds," as of many, but as of one, "And to your Seed," who is Christ. And this I say, that the law, which was four hundred and thirty years later, cannot annul the covenant that was confirmed before by God in Christ, that it should make the promise of no effect. For if the inheritance is of the law, it is no longer of promise; but God gave it to Abraham by promise. (Gal 3:16-18 NKJV)*

Under the Old Covenant, laws were given to obey, but under the New Covenant promises are given to believe in. Jesus came to the earth more than 2000 years ago to fulfill the requirements of the law, thereby canceling it and effectively nullifying the Old Covenant for believers:

> *For if that first covenant had been faultless, then no place would have been sought for a second. Because finding fault with them, He says: "Behold, the days are coming, says the LORD, when I will make a new covenant with the house of Israel and with the house of Judah - <u>not according to the covenant that I made with their fathers</u> in the day when I took them by the hand to lead them out of the land of Egypt; because they did not continue in My covenant, and I disregarded them, says the LORD. In that He says, "A new covenant," <u>He has made the first obsolete.</u> (Heb 8:7-9, 13 NKJV, emphasis added)*

Then a few hundred years later Jesus came onto the scene. Those who were still trying to live according to the Old Covenant tried to oppose Him, claiming that they were children of Abraham because of their natural descent. Jesus had something else to say to them:

> *They answered and said to Him, "Abraham is our father." Jesus said to them, "If you were Abraham's children, you would do the works of Abraham. But now you seek to kill Me, a Man who has told you the truth which I heard from God. Abraham did not do this. You are of your father the devil, and the desires of your father you want to do. He was a murderer from the beginning, and does not stand in the truth, because there is no truth in him. When he speaks a lie, he speaks from his own resources, for he is a liar and the father of it. But because I tell the truth, <u>you do not believe Me.</u> (John 8:39-40, 44-45 NKJV, emphasis added)*

Here we see clearly that these people did not believe (in) Jesus; they stubbornly refused to believe He was the Son of God. They were committing the same sin of unbelief as the Israelites hundreds of years before them in the desert! Yes Israel in the desert may have had a different "type" of unbelief (refusing to believe that God was good), but it was still unbelief in God.

The next scriptures tell us that those who believe in Jesus are sons of Abraham and are blessed along with Abraham simply because they believe.

> *Therefore know that only those who are of faith are sons of Abraham. And the Scripture, foreseeing that God would justify the Gentiles by faith, preached the gospel to Abraham beforehand, saying, "In you all the nations shall be blessed." So then those who are of faith are blessed with believing Abraham. (Gal 3:7-9 NKJV)*

> *Therefore it is of faith that it might be according to grace, so that the promise might be sure to all the seed, not only to those who are*

of the law, but also to those who are of the faith of Abraham, who is the father of us all. (Rom 4:16 NKJV)

When we understand this, it changes the way we receive from God, because we don't have to think about whether we've been good enough or too bad in order to receive from God. It changes the way we pray because we're praying *from* a place of victory, and not *for* victory. It changes the way we see God; not as a harsh being who judges us for being bad or blesses us for being good, but a loving Father that blesses simply because we believe in Jesus Christ His Son.

Law →✝→ Grace

So You Want to Preach the Law?

The only people Jesus talked "law" with were those who were heavy handed with the law. He spoke harshly with the Pharisees and the scribes who were the religious rulers of the day.

> *Then Jesus spoke to the multitudes and to His disciples, saying: "The scribes and the Pharisees sit in Moses' seat. Therefore whatever they tell you to observe, that observe and do, but do not do according to their works; for they say, and do not do. For they bind heavy burdens, hard to bear, and lay them on men's shoulders; but they themselves will not move them with one of their fingers. (Matt 23:1-4 NKJV)*

Jesus wasn't trying to get the people (including the Pharisees) to obey laws and rules more; instead He was showing the Pharisees their hypocrisy for teaching others to keep all the rules while they themselves did so poorly at keeping them.

Like many preachers today, these religious rulers were actually preaching a "watered down" version of the law, making it almost possible for them to be able to obey their own man-made rules! In reality the law is actually far more stringent than what people preach it to be! Let's take a good look at what the law actually says to people who break the law:

> *"Cursed shall you be when you come in, and cursed shall you be when you go out. The LORD will make the plague cling to you until He has consumed you from the land which you are going to possess. The LORD will strike you with consumption, with fever, with inflammation, with severe burning fever, with the sword, with scorching, and with mildew; they shall pursue you until you perish. And your Heavens which are over your head shall be*

bronze, and the earth which is under you shall be iron. The LORD will change the rain of your land to powder and dust; from the Heaven it shall come down on you until you are destroyed. Your carcasses shall be food for all the birds of the air and the beasts of the earth, and no one shall frighten them away. The LORD will strike you with the boils of Egypt, with tumors, with the scab, and with the itch, from which you cannot be healed. The LORD will strike you with madness and blindness and confusion of heart. And you shall grope at noonday, as a blind man gropes in darkness; you shall not prosper in your ways; you shall be only oppressed and plundered continually, and no one shall save you. You shall betroth a wife, but another man shall lie with her; you shall build a house, but you shall not dwell in it; you shall plant a vineyard, but shall not gather its grapes. (Deut 28:19-30 NKJV)

Actually the list goes on - take some time to read Deuteronomy 28 from verse 15 onwards. Now if people who still want to preach the law today were to actually preach the law to its full extent, they should be including all these curses as well! If a modern day preacher wanted to preach that we still have to obey the 10 Commandments, they should include in their sermon that all these curses will come upon us if we don't obey all the laws 100% of the time!

This is why the grace message sounds so radical to most people, but actually it is no more radical than the law as we can clearly see from the above verses. It's just that the law has been preached at a much reduced level and mixed up with a little bit of grace to make it sound "nice" and acceptable. But how can we ever think we can mix up or try to balance two things that are so extremely different from each other?

The Pharisees and scribes preached that people should live holy, be obedient to the laws of Moses and they also *acted* as though they were doing it themselves, but their hearts were full of evil. The Pharisees preached that as long as someone didn't commit the act of adultery, or if they weren't angry with their brother without a reason, then that person didn't break the law. But Jesus then told them that the standard of the law was actually much higher and if a person even by accident insulted their brother or entertained a single lustful thought, they were guilty of breaking *all* the other laws as well and the penalty was death. Jesus then showed them that if they wanted to preach the law, they should actually preach it to its full extent and also include all the horrifying consequences for breaking even a single law, such as death, having their hands cut off, their eyes plucked out, stoning someone who has sinned, etc. This is what Jesus meant when He made the following statements:

> *But I say to you that whoever is angry with his brother without a cause shall be in danger of the judgment... But whoever says, 'You fool!' shall be in danger of hell fire. (Matt 5:22 NKJV)*

> *"You have heard that it was said to those of old, 'You shall not commit adultery.' But I say to you that whoever looks at a woman to lust for her has already committed adultery with her in his heart. If your right eye causes you to sin, pluck it out and cast it from you; for it is more profitable for you that one of your members perish, than for your whole body to be cast into hell. And if your right hand causes you to sin, cut it off and cast it from you; for it is more profitable for you that one of your members perish, than for your whole body to be cast into hell. (Matt 5:27-30 NKJV)*

But Jesus through the cross made an end to the law, destroying for ever its constant demands of correct "behavior" and making us free to live for God because we love Him, not because we fear punishment.

> *There is no fear in love; but perfect love casts out fear, because fear involves torment. But he who fears has not been made perfect in love. (1 John 4:18 NKJV)*

Law →✝→ Grace

Why Live Holy?

The entire New Covenant speaks *against* trying to "live holy" in our own strength and be justified though our own efforts. God no longer relates to us according to our own level of obedience, but according to the perfect obedience of the One Man, Jesus Christ.

> For as by one man's disobedience [first Adam] *many were made sinners, so also by one Man's obedience* [Christ] *many will be made righteous. (Rom 5:19 NKJV, annotations added)*

Yet we see many verses in the New Covenant that still advocate a saintly lifestyle. What would be the purpose of this? Why do we still need to maintain a moral lifestyle if God's love or approval of us does not fluctuate based on how well we behave?

The verse above talks about our positional standing before God. In God's eyes, once we've put our faith in His Son Jesus Christ, we will always be justified and righteous before Him because when the Father looks at us, He sees Christ. We are *in* Christ (1 Corinthians 1:30) and nothing can ever take us out of Christ.

However, often we try and detach ourselves from Christ after we've messed up. Frequently after believers have broken their moral wings, they feel that their actions are being scrutinized by God under a magnifying glass, but this is not the case. The Father sees the perfect obedience of Jesus on our behalf! Therefore when we stumble morally, we can rest assured that God's love and approval of us remains steadfast.

On the contrary, when the Bible talks about relating to *people*, we are constantly stirred to "love one another", "keep the bond of peace", "forgive one another" etc. People are not as gracious as God and we need to maintain "good works" if we want to preserve our relationships with people, *but not with God. Note that we are not saying that people should live disobedient to God.* However the context of most scriptures in the New Covenant that talk about holy living and good works pertain to maintaining our relationships with other people. Without trying to spiritualize, let's look at some examples and interpret these scriptures for what they literally mean:

Example 1

> *Therefore, putting away lying, "Let each one of you speak truth with his neighbor," for we are members of one another. (Eph 4:25 NKJV)*

If we keep lying to people we will get into trouble sooner or later when our lies catch up with us.

Example 2

> *"Be angry, and do not sin". Do not let the sun go down on your wrath, nor give place to the devil. (Eph 4:26-27 NKJV)*

When we stay angry with someone for an extended period of time, we give the devil a foothold in our relationship with that person.

Example 3

> *Let him who stole steal no longer, but rather let him labor, working with his hands what is good, that he may have something to give him who has need. (Eph 4:28 NKJV)*

When we steal from others, it is bound to have a detrimental effect on our relationship with them when they find out. However if we work and earn money honestly, we will have enough to assist those who may have need.

Example 4

> *Let no corrupt word proceed out of your mouth, but what is good for necessary edification, that it may impart grace to the hearers. (Eph 4:29 NKJV)*

Once again this is referring to *people*, because it says our words should edify the hearers.

Example 5

> *Do not lie to one another, since you have put off the old man with his deeds, and have put on the new man who is renewed in knowledge according to the image of Him who created him, where there is neither Greek nor Jew, circumcised nor uncircumcised, barbarian, Scythian, slave nor free, but Christ is all and in all. Therefore, as the elect of God, holy and beloved, put on tender mercies, kindness, humility, meekness, longsuffering; bearing with one another, and forgiving one another, if anyone has a complaint against another; even as Christ forgave you, so you also must do. (Col 3:9-13 NKJV)*

Since we have been purged from our old sinful nature, it actually does not befit a believer to lie to his brother anymore since that would be completely contrary to the character of the Holy Spirit that now lives inside that believer. In short, it's just plain dumb to act in a manner that is contrary to one's new identity. The fruit of the Holy Spirit will permeate the life of a believer that is established in grace to such an extent that mercy, kindness, forgiveness, humility and all such divine traits will freely flow unto those around him.

There are many other examples, but I think we get the point: *God doesn't love us less when we mess up, but people do* - unless they are mature Christians that understand grace and know that nobody's behavior is perfect.

Acting According to Our New Nature

If we have died to sin (because our sinful nature was "cut" out of us through the circumcision of Christ according to Colossians 2:11), why would we want to live in it any longer? Why would we still want to run after the desires of our old sinful nature as though we haven't been cleansed from it?

> *What shall we say then? Shall we continue in sin that grace may abound? Certainly not! How shall we who died to sin live any longer in it? For he who has died has been freed from sin. Therefore do not let sin reign in your mortal body, that you should obey it in its lusts. And do not present your members as instruments of unrighteousness to sin, but present yourselves to God as being alive from the dead, and your members as instruments of righteousness to God. For sin shall not have dominion over you, for you are not under law but under grace. (Rom 6:1-2, 7, 12-14 NKJV)*

And here is how we do it: The more we try to sin less the more we will fail, because the power of sin is the law and our inability to live up to its standards:

Andre van der Merwe

> *The sting of death is sin, and the power of sin is the law. (1 Cor 15:56 NKJV)*

It is in our own efforts of trying to be holy that our greatest downfall awaits.

Our victory over the lusts of the flesh is to have our minds renewed, to have our thoughts transformed to discern the truth of God's Word and spend time in His presence, allowing Him to romance and woo us. When we begin to see how deeply His love runs for us, we will not be able to resist flowing in the fruit of the Spirit inside us, showing love and compassion to a world that needs to see Jesus.

Law →✝→ Grace

Is God Angry with Unbelievers?

All people on the face of the earth that have not put their faith in Jesus Christ as their Lord and Savior are guilty of the only sin that Jesus could *not* die for at the cross: Unbelief in Jesus.

However, contrary to popular belief, God is *not* angry with unbelievers for not accepting Him. At the cross more than 2000 years ago the sin of the whole world was forgiven and God extended His grace and kindness to *all* mankind:

> For the grace of God that brings salvation has appeared to <u>all</u> men. *(Tit 2:11 NKJV, emphasis added)*

However a person has to put their faith in this grace to receive it.

God has already reconciled the entire world to Himself through Jesus and He has made provision for every single person on the planet to be saved:

> *...that is, that God was in Christ reconciling the world to Himself, not imputing their trespasses to them, and has committed to us the word of reconciliation. (2 Cor 5:19 NKJV)*

God has already allowed all punishment against sin to be poured out on the body of Jesus and has also forgiven everybody's sin, but people have to believe in Jesus to receive this forgiveness.

Currently God is not in the punishing business anymore. In these days God is extending His goodness towards everybody on the planet (believers and unbelievers alike) because He wants them to see that He is good and that He loves them. It is the goodness of God that leads people to repentance, not a fear of punishment:

> *Or do you despise the riches of His goodness, forbearance, and longsuffering, not knowing that the goodness of God leads you to repentance? (Rom 2:4 NKJV)*

That is why atheists and sinners are not our enemies, but our friends, because if God loves them then how can we not? Our job is to show them the love of God, not judge them.

Continuing in Unbelief

However if by these people's continued unbelief they willingly reject this offer of peace from God and in the process trample the blood of Jesus underneath their feet, their hearts will all the while become more and more hardened:

> *But in accordance with your hardness and your impenitent heart you are treasuring up for yourself wrath in the day of wrath and revelation of the righteous judgment of God. (Rom 2:5 NKJV)*

On that *one single day* of judgment and not years and years as some say (see Romans 2:5 above again) these unbelievers will be judged for *not* believing in Jesus and they will have to face the dreadful consequence of spending an eternity separated from God and not *receiving* forgiveness for their sins, which is *not* God's will for *anybody* on the earth, because God loves all people!

> *For this is good and acceptable in the sight of God our Savior, who desires <u>all men</u> to be saved and to come to the knowledge of the truth. (1Tim 2:3-4 NKJV, emphasis added)*

Therefore since God loves unbelievers and wants all people to be saved, it is our mandate to extend this same love to our unbelieving neighbors, especially since we are God's hands and feet in the earth. Most unbelievers have hearts that have grown very hard, not necessarily against God, but mostly against Christians who have misrepresented God as being a harsh God who allows sickness, violence, injustice and punishment to reign on the earth. And then on top of this, if an unbeliever wants to join the church they now have to start obeying countless laws as well and they had better make sure they change their lifestyle else they will be kicked out by the church or God will punish them. Come on, what kind of person with a bit of common sense would want to sign up for that?

Let us therefore show them the kind of love that God showed us when we first came into Christ:

> *But God demonstrates His own love toward us, in that while we were still sinners, Christ died for us. (Rom 5:8 NKJV)*

None of us deserved it in the first place, why then should we try to make others feel that they have to measure up to some perfect standard?

Law →✝→ Grace

Commands In the New Covenant

The Bible is not to be considered as a set of principles to try and live up to, neither are the commands found under the New Covenant a set of orders to try and follow. By the same token though, they are also not to be seen merely as suggestions either. No, the Word of God is forever true and filled with life and power!

> For the word of God is living and powerful, and sharper than any two-edged sword, piercing even to the division of soul and spirit, and of joints and marrow, and is a discerner of the thoughts and intents of the heart. (Heb 4:12 NKJV)

However when we are given a command under the New Covenant (especially throughout books like James and Peter), this is not for us to use as a measure of how obedient we are, because this would mean that we are putting ourselves under law again and just calling it something else, namely a command.

Instead these books are to be seen as an example of what a Christian life can look like when people under the power of God manifest the fruit of the Spirit in their lives. When we live a life of praise and delight ourselves in the Lord, we are walking according to the Spirit (Romans 8:1) and we will automatically execute the commandments and manifest the fruit of the Spirit.

Unlike the Old Covenant Law, commands under the New Covenant are not to be seen as a benchmark to measure our performance against and neither can it earn us God's blessings. A key revelation that we as New Covenant believers need to have is that we have been made fully righteous and *this* forms the basis of us receiving anything from God. There is nothing that we can do that will add even a single ounce to this Godly righteousness that was imputed to us as a free gift.

It's easy to misunderstand some of the verses in the book of James if we read them in the wrong context. In the context of the New Covenant, which declares we have been saved by grace through faith (Ephesians 2:8-9), as well as the fact that we can't do anything to earn God's blessings or approval, let's look at a few of these verses:

> *But be doers of the word, and not hearers only, deceiving yourselves. (Jam 1:22 NKJV)*

> *Thus also faith by itself, if it does not have works, is dead. (Jam 2:17 NKJV)*

> *For as the body without the spirit is dead, so faith without works is dead also. (Jam 2:26 NKJV)*

These verses are not supposed to condemn us and make us feel we have not been doing enough. In fact, if any preacher ever tries to force believers into "doing more for God" by using manipulation, laying on guilt or condemnation, they are actually trying to bring people back under the Old Covenant Law!

In the Flesh or in the Spirit?

Before we tackle the three James verses however, let's quickly look at a commonly misunderstood principle:

> *There is therefore now no condemnation to those who are in Christ Jesus, who walk not according to the flesh but according to the Spirit. (Rom 8:1 NKJV)*

> *So then, those who are in the flesh cannot please God. But you are not in the flesh but in the Spirit, if indeed the Spirit of God dwells in you. Now if anyone does not have the Spirit of Christ, he is not His. (Rom 8:8-9 NKJV, emphasis added)*

When we are born again we are placed *in* Christ, but our conduct doesn't necessarily portray our true born again nature, which means we don't necessarily do everything right 100% of the time. Yet there is no condemnation, even if we don't do everything right, because Jesus has already hit the bull's eye for us! We are Christ's and God is forever pleased with us.

The Old Covenant tried to deal with the outward behavior problem, with man's sinful acts and godless deeds. But under the New Covenant God changed our hearts (He dealt with the inward problem) and when our hearts are changed, the good works will automatically follow. This is what the writer of Hebrews meant when he quoted the prophet Jeremiah:

> *Heb 10:16 This is the covenant that I will make with them after those days, says the LORD: I will put My laws into their hearts, and in their minds I will write them.*

First we have to *believe correctly* (that God loves us regardless of our performance and that we cannot earn His approval) before we will start doing the right things. Right believing will lead to right living, but simply living right in itself will not lead to right believing.

Back to the James verses, the writer is saying that if we are truly saved, there will be evidence of our faith in the form of good works. But since our minds are not fully renewed, we sometimes mess up and neglect to do the good works which God meant for us to walk in. But this is where the grace of God comes in: God does not condemn or judge or punish us if we don't do the works the writer of James talks about. He simply keeps on loving us the same.

Not to take away any of the power of James' words though. After all, what is the purpose of faith if it doesn't flow over into works? We can for example have faith that a beggar in the street should be helped by somebody else, but do nothing about it ourselves. James' writings explain what it looks like to have faith in Jesus. But these are only the elementary principles. The apostle Paul then widens our perspective on grace to demonstrate that we're not saved by works and don't live by them either - grace is what saved us and grace is what keeps us saved. But works are the *evidence* of our faith.

Let's look at what John Piper said about being judged according to our works:

"It is by grace we are saved through faith; not of ourselves, it is the gift of God. But the heart that is full of faith will overflow in attitudes and actions very different from those which flow from unbelief. Therefore, our deeds will testify truly to the genuineness or absence of faith, and it is not inconsistent for God to judge us according to our works. But we must understand that this judgment according to works does not mean we earn our salvation. Our deeds do not earn, they exhibit our salvation. Our deeds are not the merit of our righteousness, they are the mark (proof) of our new life in Christ. Our deeds are not sufficient to deserve God's favor, but they do demonstrate our faith. Please keep that distinction clear in your mind regarding our attitudes and actions: they do not earn, they exhibit; they do not merit, they mark; they do not deserve, they demonstrate. And therefore, "God will render to every man according to his deeds," including Christians."

Simply a New Law System?

The biggest difference between the Old Covenant Law and the commands found in the New Covenant is this: To be accepted and blessed by God under the Old

Covenant people *had to* obey the law. Under the New Covenant we *want to* obey the commands because we are already blessed and accepted! We cannot however devise the commands written in the New Covenant into a modern day rule keeping system, because that would mean putting ourselves under a religious scheme again, something which Paul warned against vehemently:

> *Christ has set us free to live a free life. So take your stand! Never again let anyone put a harness of slavery on you. I am emphatic about this. The moment any one of you submits to circumcision or any other rule-keeping system, at that same moment Christ's hard-won gift of freedom is squandered. (Gal 5:1-2 MSG)*

What we *can* do however is trust that the Spirit inside us will bring to completion the work that He started, stop fretting about our imperfect conduct and enjoy the life of God in us and through us. Life truly finds its purpose when we learn to simply let go and let God be Himself through us.

Law →✝→ Grace

Not Just an Old Sinner

Although it is true that all people once went by the name "sinners", the same cannot be said of a born again Christian anymore. After the crucifixion, throughout all the New Testament scriptures, the term "sinner" consistently refers to a person who has rejected God and chooses to live in subjection to the carnal desires of their sinful nature. It clearly talks about a person who has *not* been born again.

Well known grace Minister, Steve McVey (Grace Walk Ministries)[1] writes the following: *The primary project for most Christians in the modern church is to reduce the number or frequency of sins in their lives. It's a sin management program that they devote themselves to with great zeal and sincere commitment. It all sounds so good on the surface. That's the subtlety with legalism. It sounds right to the religious ear despite the fact that it contradicts and ignores what the Bible teaches. It sounds so right to some that to become godly requires that we work hard to change our bad behaviors and replace them with good ones. To them it's all about diminishing the number of sins that we commit and increasing the number of good things that we do. But Godliness doesn't come from that. Godliness is not the absence of sin. The truth is this, the reason you're godly is because the Spirit of God lives in you... Since the Holy Spirit came into your spirit, and your spirit is the core of your identity (you ARE a spirit, HAVE a soul and LIVE in a body), then you are holy, you are Godly, because God's Spirit is inside you. It doesn't have to do with resisting sin, or giving into sin. The truth is, you're just as Godly whether you sin, or don't sin. Your identity isn't established by what you do. It is established by what He has done!*

Let's look at a few examples of verses dealing with this matter in the Bible:

> *But God demonstrates His own love toward us, in that while we <u>were</u> still sinners, Christ died for us. (Rom 5:8 NKJV, emphasis added)*

This verse clearly says that while we *were* still sinners, Christ died for us, which by implication means that a believer is not a sinner anymore.

The Law is Not for Believers

> *...knowing this: that the law is not made for a righteous person, but for the lawless and insubordinate, for the ungodly and for sinners, for the unholy and profane, for murderers of fathers and murderers of mothers, for manslayers. (1 Tim 1:9 NKJV)*

There's quite a bit going on in this verse: Firstly it says that the law (including the 10 Commandments) was not made for a *righteous person*, referring to a person who has been born again and who has received the righteousness of God as a free gift, making that person perfect for ever in His eyes:

> *For by one offering he hath perfected for ever them that are sanctified. (Heb 10:14 KJV)*

Furthermore this verse says that the law was made for ungodly people and sinners and it also calls these people "lawless". That is because under the New Covenant it is not those who fail to obey the written moral code of the law that are considered to be "lawless", but instead those who refuse to accept the free gift of salvation offered by God, who turn their back on His grace and harden their hearts against the compassionate promptings of the Holy Spirit to repent and be saved. These people will retain their status as murderers, adulterers, liars and "sinners" because they refuse to accept the pardon for these sins that is freely offered by God to all those who choose to believe in Him.

Another scripture that proves this principle is the following:

> *Do you not know that the unrighteous will not inherit the kingdom of God? Do not be deceived. Neither fornicators, nor idolaters, nor adulterers, nor homosexuals, nor sodomites, nor thieves, nor covetous, nor drunkards, nor revilers, nor extortioners will inherit the kingdom of God. And such <u>were</u> some of you. But you were washed, but you were sanctified, but you were justified in the name of the Lord Jesus and by the Spirit of our God. (1 Cor 6:9-11 NKJV, emphasis added)*

Verse 9 says the "unrighteous" will not inherit the kingdom. And then it goes on to describe a list of deeds done by those who have not been forgiven their sins, in other words those who did not put their faith in Jesus to be reconciled to Him. In verse 11 however we see the key to unlock this portion of scripture: Paul says "such *were* some of you". He then goes on to describe what happened to those who put their faith in Jesus, saying they *were* cleansed and justified, meaning they now stand clean, innocent and forgiven before God. Isn't that amazing?

This serves to confirm that whenever the Bible (after the cross) talks about a sinner, it speaks about a person that has not been born again. Let's look at three more scriptures:

> *...let him know that he who turns a sinner from the error of his way will save a soul from death and cover a multitude of sins. (Jam 5:20 NKJV)*

This verse says that a "sinner" can be saved from death and his sins be forgiven if he is turned from the error of his way.

> *Now "If the righteous one is scarcely saved, where will the ungodly and the sinner appear?" (1 Pet 4:18 NKJV)*

This verse is squarely in support of 1 Timothy 1:9 (above) and it clearly contrasts the "righteous" with the "sinner and ungodly".

The next verse nails it:

> *Whoever has been born of God does not sin, for His seed remains in him; and he cannot sin, because he has been born of God. (John 3:9 NKJV)*

This confirms that a born again Christian cannot be labeled as a "sinner" according to their level of good or bad works, since it's really a no brainer that everybody makes mistakes almost every day of their lives! Yet this verse says that whoever has been born of God (born again) *cannot sin*, because their identity is not based on their level of adhering to the 10 Commandments, but instead it is based on the finished work of the cross!

Therefore we can conclude that a born again person has received the righteousness of God as a gift and has been completely sanctified (in their spirit) and can therefore not be referred to as a sinner anymore, even if their behavior does not always reflect this. Yes we do not always live in 100% obedience to God, but that does not influence the fact that God still sees us as completely righteous, forgiven, sanctified and holy. And obviously to those who believe we are saying that Christians can now just go out and sin as much as they want, *again* we are not implying this at all.

Law →✝→ Grace

Walking After the Flesh (Unrenewed Mind)

Previously we concluded a two part series on why Christians still sometimes struggle with the works that the law labels as "sin". Under the New Covenant however, all the sins (past present and future) of a believer have been forgiven:

> *I write to you little children, because your sins are forgiven you for His name's sake. (1 John 2:12 NKJV)*

> *…then He adds, "Their sins and their lawless deeds I will remember no more. (Heb 10:17 NKJV)*

We concluded previously that Christians sometimes still make mistakes mainly because of two reasons, namely because of an unrenewed mind and also because of external temptations. Our body will simply yield itself as an instrument to whichever part we give control to:

1) To our 100% righteous born again spirit man, or

2) to the unrenewed part of our mind. If the mind is unrenewed, it will be at enmity (war) with our spirit. The body will follow like a slave to whichever one of these two we yield control to.

If our mind has been renewed by the washing of the Word of God, we will use our body as an instrument of righteousness. But if a person walks after the lusts of their unrenewed mind (flesh), their body will be a slave to sin and reap the carnal (earthly) consequences of that sin. Yes earthly consequences, because all the eternal punishment was dealt with at the cross.

Buckle up because here's a radical statement: because *New Covenant believers are no longer the law, they can't essentially break the law and therefore can technically speaking no longer commit "sin"*, certainly no sin that they can be judged or condemned for.

> *...for where there is no law, there is no transgression. (Rom 4:15b NKJV)*

Actually they are not committing sins, but rather "works of the flesh".

> *Now the works of the flesh are evident, which are: adultery, fornication, uncleanness, lewdness, idolatry, sorcery, hatred, contentions, jealousies, outbursts of wrath, selfish ambitions, dissensions, heresies, envy, murders, drunkenness, revelries... (Gal 5:19-21 NKJV)*

When believers and unbelievers mess up, we class their actions differently. Indulgence in immorality by these two different groups can be described like this:

Believers: *Works of the flesh (flesh = unrenewed part of the believer's mind)*

Unbelievers: *Sins*

This is not just word play, because an incorrect understanding about *why* a Christian still slips up from time to time serves to contribute towards the misconception of believers seeing themselves being caught up in the unbreakable grip of sin, whereas they have actually been set free from it through grace:

> *For sin shall not have dominion over you, for you are not under law but under grace. (Rom 6:14 NKJV)*

We can clearly see from the listed "works of the flesh" in Galatians 5 (above) that if a person were to practice such things on a regular basis, they will very quickly not only estrange themselves from the people who love them, but also ought to find themselves in jail when the local authorities and law systems catch up with them for things like theft, murder, etc. (It's interesting that the Bible lists hatred and jealousy up there with *murder*).

When someone is punished like this by their local law system or scorned by the people around them for misconduct, these are the *earthly* consequences for their actions which include the anger, condemnation and resentment of the people they have harmed because unlike God, people have *not* yet forgiven us for all our mistakes past, present and future. People aren't as gracious as God and therefore when we harm people and trespass against them, we need to confess to them and ask for their forgiveness.

> *Confess your trespasses to one another, and pray for one another, that you may be healed. (Jam 5:16 NKJV)*

It's well worth noting at this point that even though a *believer* that practices such things might at some point face the music with people or with their local authorities, God will never resent them or stop loving them, even when they commit the most horrendous thing. The grace of God has made provision enough to cover even the biggest sin:

> ...*But where sin abounded, grace abounded much more. (Rom 5:20b NKJV)*

Now someone might ask "But why would God still want to love such a person even if they have committed these horrible things?" The answer is simply that once a person has been born again and they are now *in* Christ:

> *But of Him you are in Christ Jesus, who became for us wisdom from God - and righteousness and sanctification and redemption. (1 Cor 1:30 NKJV, emphasis added)*

Because of this, the Father loves them the same as Christ. Nothing can ever separate them from God's love. God is not ignorant of our mistakes, but His indignation against the sinful condition of man was fully appeased by the perfect sacrifice of His Son.

Trying to Live More "Holy"

Something that New Covenant believers should guard against, is trying in their own effort to "live more holy". Sanctification does not mean we try to stop doing this or that sin; sanctification simply means living from our position in Christ. When we try to "become" more holy, we go back under the law and open up the door for condemnation to come in when we make mistakes, making us aware of our own shortcomings and robbing us again of our confidence before God. We will then not *want* to get to know God because we'd feel too guilty to talk to Him.

The implication of this is that we will just have an ordinary life and live like practical atheists whose lives are void of any of the power of our mighty God. We will continue to feed our unbelief and not have our minds renewed and therefore we will not get to know God for who He really is: a kind and gracious Father who is always poised towards blessing and prospering us beyond our wildest dreams.

Cornel Marais from Charisma Ministries[1] says: *"Just remember that when you go back and live under law as a saved believer, it doesn't mean you've lost your salvation, it just means you might only get to know God when you die, so don't blame Him for your powerless religious existence on earth while you refuse to get to know Him."*

Law →✝→ Grace

Will Obeying the Law Give Me Victory Over Sin?

> *For sin shall not have dominion over you, for you are not under law but under grace. (Rom 6:14 NKJV)*

The law controlled us and kept us under its power until the time came when we would have faith. In fact, the law was supposed to be our teacher until we put our faith in Jesus. But now that we have put our faith in Jesus, we don't need this teacher (the law) anymore:

> *But before faith came, we were kept under guard by the law, kept for the faith which would afterward be revealed. Therefore the law was our tutor to bring us to Christ, that we might be justified by faith. But after faith has come, we are no longer under a tutor. (Gal 3: 23-25 NKJV)*

The law demands that we live a perfectly holy life 100% of the time. Failure to comply will result in punishment and death. *These requirements will never change.* The law is what it is and grace cannot change the law's mind. The only way to come out from under the law is to die to the law.

> *Therefore, my brethren, you also have become dead to the law through the body of Christ, that you may be married to another - to Him who was raised from the dead, that we should bear fruit to God. (Rom 7:4 NKJV)*

> *For I through the law died to the law that I might live to God. (Gal 2:19 NKJV)*

Trying to obey the law will only end up in breaking the law, because nobody on the face of the earth can obey the law 100% of the time. Nobody ever could, except Jesus Christ. Grace also does not enable us to keep the law. Rather grace enables us to live and feed from the life of God of which He has made us partakers, filling us with His mighty Holy Spirit. Any good works that flow from us as a result of this is simply a fruit of the Spirit inside us, so we really have nothing to boast about.

The Bible says the strength of sin is the law, because it is only through the law that we know what sin is. It is the law that brought sin to life!

> *What shall we say then? Is the law sin? Certainly not! On the contrary, I would not have known sin except through the law. For I would not have known covetousness unless the law had said, "You shall not covet." But sin, taking opportunity by the commandment, produced in me all manner of evil desire. I was alive once without the law, but when the commandment came, sin revived and I died. And the commandment, which was to bring life, I found to bring death. (Rom 7:7-10 NKJV)*

> *Moreover the law entered that the offense might abound. (Rom 5:20a NKJV)*

> *The sting of death is sin, and the strength of sin is the law. (1 Cor 15:56 NKJV)*

> *Therefore by the deeds of the law no flesh will be justified in His sight, for by the law is the knowledge of sin. (Rom 3:20 NKJV)*

But how then are we supposed to live in obedience? If we don't have any standard to measure our performance by, how can we know that we are really obeying God? The answer is simpler than we may think: By simply believing in Jesus and the victory He has obtained for us.

> *For whatever is born of God overcomes the world. And this is the victory that has overcome the world - our faith. (1 John 5:4 NKJV)*

It is through faith that we please God, not by trying to live more holy:

> *But without faith it is impossible to please Him. (Heb 11:6a NKJV)*

> *And the law is not of faith... (Gal 3:12a NKJV)*

Combining these last two verses we see that we cannot please God by trying to live according to the law.

Now we may also ask: "What are we then supposed to do? Doesn't God expect us to *do* something?" There were some people that asked Jesus the exact same question:

> *Then they said to Him, "What shall we do, that we may work the works of God?" Jesus answered and said to them, "This is the work of God, that you believe in Him whom He sent". (John 6:28-29 NKJV)*

Our faith is stirred when we spend time in the presence of God and have supernatural encounters with Him, when we worship Him, when we experience the fulfillment of seeing heaven kiss earth, when we receive revelation that renews our mind and when we hear Him speak to us:

> *So then <u>faith comes by hearing</u>, and hearing by the word of God. (Rom 10:17 NKJV, emphasis added)*

When we experience these things, a natural result will be victory over sin, good works and a holy lifestyle motivated by love for God. That's why it's called the "fruit" of the Spirit.

Jesus Preached the Law

Jesus talked mostly about the law only to people who were heavily under the influence of the law. He was not encouraging them to try and obey the law more; instead He was showing them that they were hypocrites for teaching others to keep all the laws while they themselves could not do it either.

In Luke 18 a rich young ruler asked Jesus what he should do to inherit eternal life. This was the man's first mistake. He wanted to *do* something to inherit eternal life, believing he could earn it. Jesus, realizing that this man was relying heavily on obeying the law for his salvation, answered him:

> *You know the commandments: 'Do not commit adultery,' 'Do not murder,' 'Do not steal,' 'Do not bear false witness,' 'Honor your father and your mother.'" And he* [the rich young ruler] *said, "All these things I have kept from my youth." So when Jesus heard these things, He said to him, "You still lack one thing. Sell all that you have and distribute to the poor, and you will have treasure in Heaven; and come, follow Me." But then he heard this, he became very sorrowful, for he was very rich. (Luke 18:20-23 NKJV, annotations added)*

Jesus simply showed the man that however well he thought he may have been keeping the law, he would always fall short. The law will always tell us that we have not done enough, that we need to accomplish more; to be more holy and to perform better. Trying to obey the law will never give people victory over sin - it will only show them how far they fall short. But praise be to God, there was one man who did it *all* on our behalf: Jesus Christ!

Our key verse for this chapter implies that as long as we try to live under the law, sin will have dominion over us.

> *For sin shall not have dominion over you, for you are not under law but under grace. (Rom 6:14 NKJV)*

However when we come out from under the law, realizing that there is now a better way to live, namely by faith, we are enabled to achieve victory over all those bad habits and mistakes we kept on making while living under the law. Now is that powerful or what?

Law →✝→ Grace

Misunderstood Bible Terminology

In this chapter we'll take a close look at some Bible terminology that can easily be misunderstood if not read through the perspective of the New Covenant. Many of these verses, especially from the epistles of the apostle John, have been used as a whip to beat the church back into obeying the Old Covenant Law. A good understanding of grace and righteousness would go a long way into clearing up the fog surrounding these topics of discussion, such as the terms "fellowship", "practicing truth", "committing sin" or "lawlessness", etc. Undivided attention and prolonged concentration is strongly recommended for this one.

Fellowship

It is commonly believed that whenever a believer messes up in regard to their moral behavior, that they fall out of fellowship with God and that they need to confess their sins in order to restore such "fellowship". However when viewed from this perspective the term "fellowship" (better known as "fellowshipping with God" in Pentecostal circles) would then refer to a feeling of intimacy that comes and goes depending on our ability to perform at our best. This is not what scripture has to say, in fact not even once in the entire New Testament is the word "fellowship" described in this manner, especially when it pertains to our relationship with God. The term "fellowshipping with God" is not even used once in the entire Bible. It is a phrase that has been conjured up by people to refer to their own quiet time with God and through the last few decades it has been twisted by legalists to make believers feel guilty and stand accused of being "out of fellowship" with God if they didn't allocate a certain amount of time per week to prayer and Bible study. On the contrary, here are a few examples of how the word "fellowship" has been used in Biblical terms:

> *...For what fellowship has righteousness with lawlessness? And what communion has light with darkness? And what accord has Christ*

with Belial? Or what part has a believer with an unbeliever? (2 Cor 6:14b-15 NKJV)

Take note how these opposing entities are contrasted with each other: righteousness vs. lawlessness, light vs. darkness, Christ (anointed) vs. Belial (worthless) and believer vs. unbeliever. It says that such opposites cannot have *fellowship* with one another, meaning they are not compatible. Just as Christ cannot have fellowship with Belial, in the same way a believer is not to be considered by the same measure as an unbeliever. If a person is therefore out of fellowship with Christ it means that they have *not been born again* and they fall under the same category as darkness, Belial and lawlessness in the above verse.

God is faithful, by whom you were called into the fellowship of His Son, Jesus Christ our Lord. (1 Cor 1:9 NKJV)

We *were* called *into* the fellowship and therefore when we put our faith in Christ we *are* now *in* the fellowship.

If we say that we have fellowship with him, and walk in darkness, we lie and do not practice the truth. (1 John 1:6 NKJV)

This verse makes it abundantly clear that the apostle John is talking about our position in Christ, not our behavior. *We cannot say that we have fellowship with God* (in other words that we have been born again) *if we walk in darkness* (which means we have not actually been born again), because then we would be lying. In simple English: You cannot say you are a Christian if you have not been born again!!

Practicing Truth or Righteousness / Walking in Darkness

Now of course the pessimist or legalist would say, "Yes but what about the parts in the previous verse that says "*walk* in darkness" and "*practice* the truth?" The answer is simple: once again this is not referring to our own works of righteousness; in fact it has nothing to do with our behavior. The terminology used by the apostle John for being born again is to "practice righteousness" or "practice truth" or "walk in the light" (we will deal with "walking in the light" a little later).

If you know that He is righteous, you know that everyone who practices righteousness is born of Him. (1 John 2:29 NKJV)

We know for a fact that every believer on the planet messes up from time to time. It's clear therefore that the above verse can't be referring to our behavior, because this would imply that anybody who makes a mistake is not born of God.

In contrast, when John talks about those who "commit sin" or who "practice lawlessness" or "walk in darkness" he is referring to the unsaved. *This principle stays consistent throughout all 3 of John's epistles.* Predominantly however these verses have been read through a legalistic point of view, causing much perplexity in the body of Christ.

Committing Sin or Lawlessness

Another shining example is 1 John 3:4-9:

> *Whoever commits sin also commits lawlessness, and sin is lawlessness. And you know that He was manifested to take away our sins, and in Him there is no sin. (1 John 3:4-5 NKJV)*

Once again John is referring to the unsaved here. Whenever the New Testament refers to those who "commit sin" or "practice lawlessness" it does *not* have the same meaning as under the Old Testament when people were still judged according to the law. The only sin in the New Testament is *not* believing in Jesus, as we also saw previously when we talked about "The Unforgivable Sin".

Verse 5 (above) depicts God's answer to mankind's problem of sin - He took our sin away and placed us *in* Christ where we now are completely forgiven and seen as though we've never even committed a single sin! Read verse 5 again in this context. Is the light beginning to go on yet that John is not talking about our behavior in this epistle?

> *Whoever abides in Him does not sin. Whoever sins has neither seen Him nor known Him. (1 John 3:6 NKJV)*

This verse mentions another "buzz" concept, namely to "abide" in Him. It's really very simple to prove that *this also refers to being saved* and not to our own efforts to maintain a good standing with God. Simply do searches for the word "abide(s)" on any Bible software program and study the results.

This verse further says that whoever sins "has not seen God or does not know God", which implies not having a relationship with Him. Many (if not all) sincere Christians who have had an intimate relationship with God for decades still make mistakes every day of their lives despite their best efforts. If this verse meant that they are disqualified from their relationship with God if they sin even once (because it doesn't say "sin a hundred times" or "sin four times per day"), this would amount to *no one on the entire planet* being able to maintain a stable relationship with God. Clearly therefore this is not the context of this verse. Let's look at the subsequent three verses:

⁷ Little children, let no one deceive you. He who practices righteousness [which means to be saved] *is righteous, just as He* [God] *is righteous. ⁸ He who sins* [an unbeliever] *is of the devil, for the devil has sinned from the beginning. For this purpose the Son of God was manifested, that He might destroy the works of the devil. ⁹ Whoever has been born of God* [a believer] *does not sin, for His* [God's] *seed remains in him; and he cannot sin, because he has been born of God. (1 John 3:7-9 NKJV, annotations added)*

The key here is verse 9. How is it possible that a believer cannot sin if we're all too aware of how many mistakes we make? Simply because John is not talking about our behavior! He is still using the same terminology to differentiate between being saved or not. Read verses 7 - 9 again and let it sink in. In verse 8, if John meant that anybody who commits an *act* of sin is of the devil, it would imply that all Christians are of the devil. Clearly this is not what he meant.

There are two main reasons why Christians can't be called "sinners" anymore, the first being because they are no longer under the Old Covenant Law. And since there is no more law to break (and sin is defined as breaking the law) consequently their mistakes can no longer be called "sinning".

And where there is no law there is no transgression. (Rom 4:15b NKJV)

Secondly everybody on the planet falls into one of two categories: they're either a sinner or a saint. Not once in the entire Bible is mention made of a "neutral" position somewhere in the middle. We either have God as our Father, or the devil. So a person is either a saint or they're a sinner. A Christian can't be a sinner.

Practicing Lawlessness or Unrighteousness

Jesus basically used the exact same terminology in Matthew 7:15 when He warned about the false prophets that would come in sheep's clothing. What most people miss though is that down in verse 21 He is *still* talking about these same people. We'll look at the entire text here so the skeptics can see for themselves:

"Beware of false prophets, who come to you in sheep's clothing, but inwardly they are ravenous wolves. You will know them by their fruits. Do men gather grapes from thornbushes or figs from thistles? Even so, every good tree bears good fruit, but a bad tree bears bad fruit. A good tree cannot bear bad fruit, nor can a bad tree bear good fruit. Every tree that does not bear good fruit is cut down and thrown into the fire. Therefore by their fruits you will know them. (Matt 7:15-20 NKJV)

These verses pertain specifically to the fact that an unbeliever cannot manifest the fruit of the Holy Spirit because they don't have the Spirit living in them. They may act kindly or behave in a very moral manner, but their hearts still remain evil and sinful, hence Jesus says they are "ravenous wolves" on the inside.

Also, since Jesus is the tree of life and the good vine, He cannot bear bad fruit. This means that we as believers are the good fruit that He bears since His life is recreated in us. God the Father sowed His own Son and reaped more sons.

Now note that in the next verses that Jesus is *still* talking about these same people (the false prophets and unbelievers):

> *"Not everyone who says to Me, 'Lord, Lord,' shall enter the kingdom of Heaven, but he who does the will of My Father in Heaven. Many will say to Me in that day, 'Lord, Lord, have we not prophesied in Your name, cast out demons in Your name, and done many wonders in Your name?' And then I will declare to them, 'I never knew you; depart from Me, you who practice lawlessness!' (Matt 7:21-23 NKJV)*

In verse 21 Jesus says that "whoever does the will of the Father" shall enter the kingdom of heaven. Now hang in there for the next paragraph; it may seem disjointed, but we will pull it all together at the end.

In the gospel of John, Jesus also said the following:

> *Jesus answered, "Most assuredly, I say to you, unless one is born of water and the Spirit, he cannot enter the kingdom of God. That which is born of the flesh is flesh, and that which is born of the Spirit is spirit. Do not marvel that I said to you, 'You must be born again'. (John 3:5-7 NKJV)*

Here Jesus was referring to the two different births (natural and spiritual) of any human being that enters the kingdom of heaven – firstly they are born from the water of their mother's womb (He was *not* talking about water baptism, because in verse 6 He specifically talks about being born of the "flesh" which means to be born into this world) and secondly they are born of the spirit, better known as being "born again". Now what does the Bible teach us about how to be born again?

> *...that if you confess with your mouth the Lord Jesus and believe in your heart that God has raised Him from the dead, you will be saved. For with the heart one believes unto righteousness, and with the mouth confession is made unto salvation. (Rom 10:9-10 NKJV)*

Once again it would "appear" as though we have a contradiction: In Matthew 7:21 Jesus says that whoever *does the will* of the Father shall enter the kingdom of heaven, but from John 3:5 and Romans 10:9-10 we can conclude that whoever *believes in Jesus* shall enter the kingdom of heaven.

The following verse sheds some light on what it means to "do" the will of the Father and "work" the works of God:

> *Jesus answered and said to them, "This is the work of God, that you believe in Him whom He sent". (John 6:29 NKJV)*

As before we see that these expressions, even though they appear to imply that we have to do some external action or work, actually refers to an action of faith, of placing our trust in Jesus Christ. This is what it means to do the will of the Father.

Then in Matthew 7:23 Jesus tells those who "practice lawlessness" to depart from Him, referring to the unsaved again, just like we previously saw John do in his epistles. Jesus also said to them "I never knew you". Can it be any clearer that in fact He was referring to unbelievers? Practicing lawlessness does not mean breaking the 10 Commandments: *it means not being saved*.

Obeying Commandments

Let's slam another nail in the coffin and prove to the legalists just how fully the grace of God has made provision for our natural human insufficiencies. Let's try and figure this one out together. Remembering all that we have just learnt about those who "practice righteousness" and previously also about those who "commit sin", it is obvious that John could also be talking about something else than obeying the 10 Commandments when he says that we need to "obey God's commandments". This is in fact a big favorite with those who still preach that we should live according to the Old Testament Laws. Let's take a look and see what John really meant:

> *Now by this we know that we know Him, if we keep His commandments. He who says, "I know Him," and does not keep His commandments, is a liar, and the truth is not in him. (1 John 2:3-4 NKJV)*

Some other verses address this same issue and the aforementioned "abiding in Him" issue as well:

> *Now he* [someone] *who keeps His* [God's] *commandments abides in Him, and He in him. And by this we know that He abides*

> *in us, by the Spirit whom He has given us. (1 John 3:24 NKJV, annotations added)*

From Paul's letter to the Ephesians we know that every believer receives and is *sealed* with the Holy Spirit as a guarantee that they are indeed saved:

> *In Him you also trusted, after you heard the word of truth, the gospel of your salvation; in whom also, having believed, you were sealed with the Holy Spirit of promise, who is the guarantee of our inheritance until the redemption of the purchased possession, to the praise of His glory. (Eph 1:13-14 NKJV)*

We can therefore see that believers receive the Holy Spirit as a guarantee after they are born again and because He is *sealed* inside them He naturally will also "abide" with them and they with Him. Now in this context, read 1 John 3:24 (above) again. Clearly John is saying that whosoever has the Holy Spirit (a believer), such a person also keeps God's commandments. What "commandments" is he talking about?

> *And this is His commandment: that we should believe on the name of His Son Jesus Christ and love one another, as He gave us commandment. (1 John 3:23 NKJV)*

When the very nature and character of the person of the Holy Spirit resides within a person, a natural result will be that they begin to change in their outward behavior. People will begin to notice a difference in the way they live. It can't happen the other way round – somebody that acts in a well behaving manner can never through their good actions be changed on the inside – they need to receive the Holy Spirit first. This is exactly what the apostle John is talking about: When we believe in God and are born again, we will love one another more and more as a fruit of the Holy Spirit that abides within us. *Obeying God's commandments in the New Testament therefore means to believe in Jesus.*

Walking in the Light

> *But if we walk in the light as He is in the light, we have fellowship with one another, and the blood of Jesus His Son cleanses us from every sin. (1 John 1:7 NKJV)*

At a first glance, this verse seems to say that as long as we hold up our end of the bargain, Jesus' blood will cleanse us from our sin. However to walk in the light as God is in the light is actually a result of God giving us *His* righteousness - again John is talking about our secure position in Christ here, not our behavior. Our position in Christ is eternally secured the day we put our faith in Jesus Christ as our Lord and Savior. From that day on we "walk in the light".

Now some people may ask: "What is light?" In John 8:12 Jesus said "I am the light of the world", therefore we can conclude Jesus is light. When we are born again we are placed *in* Christ (1 Corinthians 1:30, Ephesians 2:10) and therefore *we* are in the light. But because we are *in* the light, we also become light:

> *...you were once darkness, but now* <u>*you are light*</u> *in the Lord. Walk as children of light. (Eph 5:8 NKJV, emphasis added)*

Jesus also says we are the light of the world:

> *You are the light of the world. A city that is set on a hill cannot be hidden. (Matt 5:14 NKJV)*

As He was (and still is) the light, so we have become as He is:

> *...because as he is so also are we in this world. (1 John 4:17b NKJV)*

Most of the arguments against the grace message come from the three epistles of John. Most legalists that read these books see it as a set of instructions that tell us what we are supposed to do, instead of reading it in the correct context (as we've already discussed previously): The epistles of John were written by John to his "little children" who had just come out from under the false teachings of Gnostics. John was by no means trying to tell them to "DO THIS!" or "DO THAT!" Instead he was telling them how secure they were in Christ, assuring them of their eternal salvation.

1 John 1:7 (above) says the blood cleanses from *every* sin and to any sensible believer that should pretty much mean exactly what it says: *every* sin. In the original Greek language the word that was used for "cleanses" was *katharizo*. This literally means to "continually cleanse". So if we make a mistake the blood removes it completely and this happens day and night without ceasing. Also if we believe we can "walk in the light" based on our own obedience, why then would we need the blood to continually cleanse us? Because now we are doing it all our self! No, we walk in the light because we have been given the righteousness of God as a free gift. Here are some more verses to explain this:

> *For you were once darkness, but now you are light in the Lord...*
> *(Eph 5:8a NKJV, emphasis added)*

This says that we were once lost (in darkness), but now we have been born again (we have become light).

> *And the city had no need of the sun, nor of the moon, that they might shine in it, for the glory of God illuminated it, and its lamp is the Lamb. And the nations of those who are saved will walk in the light of it; and the kings of the earth bring their glory and honor into it. (Rev 21:23-24 NKJV, emphasis added)*

This passage says that *those who have been saved* will walk in the light. Once again "walking in the light" refers to the believer's secure position in Christ and not to some physical thing they are supposed to do.

Yes when we look at our behavior we will clearly see that we make mistakes every day and that we don't necessarily walk in the light in our actions, but that is because our minds have not yet been fully renewed. Until the day we go to be with the Lord there will always be some area in our lives that we will need to bring under submission to the authority of God, whether it be thought patterns, habits, or whatever. The point is that we don't practice "correct behavior" in order to earn God's approval, but it happens spontaneously as a result of us falling more in love with Jesus and becoming more and more aware of how wonderfully we have been saved.

During our entire time spent on the earth we will always be able to improve our external conduct and bring it more in line with our perfect position in Christ. But until we receive our glorified bodies, God has already provided more than enough grace to cover any mistakes we may make along the way. There is nothing wrong with living moral lives, but we should not use our ability to live ethically as the measure or standard of our relationship with God.

Law →✝→ Grace

To Wrap Things Up - Personal Conclusion

While working full time as a Mechanical Engineer, I wrote this book over a period of two years. It then took another year to beat my rough drafts into shape, have it proof read and edit it another 200 times before submitting it for printing.

It was only through the looking glass of Grace that the Bible began to make sense. Interpreting the scriptures in any other way will always leave us with hundreds of questions, continual anxiety about our eternal security, depression about our wellbeing and make us question whether God is *really* as good as we suspect He may be…

I may have come over a bit too strong at times, but I'm still getting over the damage done to me by religion over a period of more than two decades of my life. I'm also living to see others set free in the same way! Traditions, rule keeping and religious routine can never be a substitute for the vibrant, passionate, intimate and personal relationship that Father wants to have with each of us.

Once I jumped into this river, there was no turning back. I can never go back to trying to relate to God under that old, strict, regimented way of life. Grace is progressively saturating our church meetings, circles of influence, families and homes, everybody coming into the passionate, liberating, superior, unashamed and powerful sphere of freedom! I'm part of a community of people who are excited about what Abba is doing across the earth, lightening up the countenance of His bride with the undiluted revelation of His unconditional love!

I highly recommend visiting the websites of the ministries listed on the next page and subscribing to their newsletters, downloading their sermons and soaking in the powerful truths contained therein. Also remember to subscribe to the free bi-weekly newsletters from www.NewCovenantGrace.com and watch this space for more books coming in the near future, tackling topics such as:

Andre van der Merwe

- Can Christians Lose Their Salvation?

- Do We Need to Ask God for More Faith?

- Why Grace Doesn't Appeal to Legalists

- Seated With Christ in Heaven… Right Now!

- Church Leadership

- Is God in Control?

- Universalism (Ultimate Salvation)

- The "External God" Phenomenon

- And much more!

Internet Links

Foreword
1) http://ccihk.com
2) http://www.freedomlife.org.au
3) http://www.NewCovenantGrace.com

Matt 5:17-18 – Did Jesus End the Law or Not?
1) http://www.wordofhisgrace.org
2) http://en.wikipedia.org/wiki/613_Mitzvot

The Law Arouses Sin
1) http://newnaturepublications.com

Righteousness Through the Law Pt 1
1) http://en.wikipedia.org/wiki/Pharisees

Do Christians Need to Repent?
1) http://www.ibethel.org

Powerless Religion
1) http://en.wikipedia.org/wiki/Crusades
2) http://en.wikipedia.org/wiki/Renaissance
3) http://en.wikipedia.org/wiki/Protestant_Reformation
4) http://ccihk.com

Tithes and Offerings
1) http://www.dynamicministries.com

The Importance of Our Thoughts
1) http://www.awmi.net/extra/audio/1047

Do Christians Need to Confess Their Sins? Pt 2 (1 John 1:9)
1) http://en.wikipedia.org/wiki/Gnosticism
2) http://escapetoreality.org
3) http://ccihk.com
4) http://www.freedomlife.org.au

If this truth about confessing our sins to God is still unclear, it would help a great deal to download the sermon called "Do Christians have to confess their sins to God?" by Rob Rufus from City Church International in Hong Kong. Simply follow this link (the date of the sermon is 8 June 2008): http://www. citychurchinternational.net/2008.html

Not Just an Old Sinner
1) http://www.gracewalk.org

Walking After the Flesh (Unrenewed Mind)
1) http://www.charismaministries.org

Acknowledgements

Andre would like to thank:

My wife Natalie – even before we got married I saw the depth of your indescribable love for people. I'm forever grateful to be the fortunate beneficiary of receiving that love every day of my life. You are all I ever wanted in a woman. I am so very proud of you. To my little Zoe, daddy loves you so very much. Thank you for coloring in our lives the way you do.

My mom and dad (Frans and Tiena) - thank you for your love over the years and for teaching me responsibility and discipline. Your care has shielded me from much harm and I will love you always.

My sister, Lumari - My little sis I will always love you. What a privilege it is to see God transform your life through Grace. Always be yourself, you are a firestarter!

Paul Ellis - Hope I get to meet you some day my friend. You are a MASSIVE inspiration to me. Your writings and wisdom have impacted me in so many ways - thank you.

Morne (Major) - Your free life has mentored me for years. Thank you for your sincerity, all the laughs, our talks on the golf courses and for never allowing your heart to be tamed. I love you my brother.

All the grace warriors and kingdom carriers that have influenced my life, some of whom I personally know (and this list is by no means exhaustive): Joseph Prince, Bill Johnson, Curry Blake, Andrew and Jamie Wommack, Cornel and Rensia Marais, Rob and Glenda Rufus, Andrew Farley, Tony and Robyn Ide, Richard Gamel, Clifford Nathan, Paul Ellis, Ryan and Laura Rhoades, Bertie Brits, Brandon Lee, Craig and Dawn Glenn, Ryan and Kylie Rufus, Steve and Gina Barker, Chad and Jaye Mansbridge, Wayne and Jennifer Duncan, Steve McVey, Art Henkel, Charolotte Cronk (Mom), Neels Labuschagne, Joe van den Berg, Andre Bronkhorst, Henk and Sandra - You are an inspiration to me and I thank Abba Father for leading us down this road of freedom, power, life, joy and love! Keep fighting the good fight, the wave of grace is flooding the earth!

Andre and Natalie would like to thank:

Abba Father - Your unfolding plan and endless goodness have revealed to us your true nature. Thank you for ambushing us in Hong Kong. We look forward to the next adventure and growing in our knowledge of truth. Your faithfulness is boundless, Your plans for us abound in goodness. We love every moment!

Our mom and dad (Braam and Elise) - We love you very much and thank you for your help, honesty and encouragement. Thank you for running this race with us and motivating us to stay the course. We trust that unfailing love will continue to reveal Himself to you in faithfulness.

Our brothers and sisters (Dirk, Anita, Petrus and also Andy) - Thank you for always loving us. We enjoy our times together and couldn't have wished for better siblings. We love you.

Rob and Glenda - We owe you our lives. Were it not for your obedience we would never have been liberated this way. We continue to miss you greatly our spiritual mom and dad. Your passion has ignited far greater fires than you can imagine and your legacy is abounding.

All our other friends at CCI (Johnny, Sophie, Marina, Ryan, Kylie, Ash, Adele, Steve, Gina, Jonathan, Annerine, Milly, Simon, Christy, Jorike, Noelise, Bonnie, Candice, Kirsten, Dale, Ruth, Tony the Greek, Theresa, Lillian, Dave, Helen, Sarah, Annelize (wish we'd met you), Neil, Audrey, Rob, Bobsy, John, Chris, Elmien, Lex, Marike, and all you other happy people) - It was a thrilling run we had with you guys! You are legends and forerunners of the revolution! Steve, I valued our chats and squash games immensely – you continue to be a great source of inspiration to me and a close brother I can count on. Johnny I miss you my brother!

Tony and Robyn - Thank you for taking us under your wings and being our family so far from our home country. If there is one thing we have learnt from you it is to walk in love. And how refreshing has it been to discover love's diversity! We love you guys and keep you in our hearts.

Our Oz family at Freedom Life (Clayton, Taryn, Warren, Nicola, Thinus, Bianca, Tony the Greek again (been continent hopping with us hey?), Lucian, Kim, Charles, Bridgette, Fernand, Stewart, Rona, Dale Tracy, Brad, Melissa, Luke, Simon, Liz, Joe, Shaun, Leo, Ross, Yvonne x 2, Richard, Kaye, Peter, Kaye, Simon, Brooke, Nic, Kirsty, Michelle, Trevor, Lisa, Greg, Aubrey, Mandy, Melissa and boys, Veronica, Peter, Shane and all you others) and also Henk - words simply cannot describe the love and affection we felt from you guys. We found a home in Perth among you and we miss you heaps. Clayton my china, your passion is addictive - keep going for it! Thinus my boet, we will definitely light a few braaivleis fires in the near future, love you heaps! Warren, your boldness and dedication to make a difference speak volumes of your heart. Keep standing for truth. Luke your wisdom and compassion is infectious, love you heaps bro! Michael, wish we could have gotten to know you better - the four walls of a building seems to be getting too small for you as well. Keep going for it bro! Charles and Kim, He will lead you into all truth. Love you guys! Trev and Mishy Moo we loved our times with you! Mwah! Tracy and Dale thanks for your genuine care and love, miss you guys. To all the girls, you are sorely missed, what a blessing to have you as sisters! You made us feel like royalty.

Des and Carien - Hope your journey is filled with love and adventure. We love and miss you.

Hein - Thank you for being a true friend all these years. We love you.

Judy - You are a true gem. We admire and love you so much. Your dedication, sincerity and love inspire all who know you.

Cornel and Rensia - We could write an entire book about you two. It has meant the world to us having you by our side through this journey of discovery. You remain deeply loved and missed over here. Bless you for standing up for truth Cornel. Your ministry has touched countless lives.

Janelie - Love you heaps our angel friend! Your gentle spirit ministers love and compassion to all your friends.

Adri Marie - Words are not enough to describe what we share with you. You are a breath of life, a river in the desert, a welcome home sign. We love you.

Melanie - You are a faithful steward of your gifts. Keep rocking on!

Kobus - You are a ninja, a wild untamed warrior! Love you to bits! Your passion for Grace is highly addictive and we know Abba will open those doors at the tight time. You mean a lot to us buddy; you are one of our favorites.

Fran and Tiana - Wow you guys rock! We are looking so very much forward to sharing this life of God with you. Love you lots! Thanks for the awesome book cover design Tiana! (To anybody needing graphic design work done, you can e-mail Tiana (from HEARTWIRE CREATIVE) at tianavntr@gmail.com

Johannes and Deidre - You've trodden some of the deepest tracks in our hearts. We love you so much. Wow we've been through so much together and we can't wait for the rest! You are a safe haven for many people.

Rocco and Amanda - We value your friendship tremendously, love you lots.

All our other buddies (sorry if we forgot to mention you): Lenandi, Perry and Melanie, Deon (Belpel), Mike, Jo and Tish, Retha (Grace Stalker), Este (Ketter), Esmarie, Ewald, Nadia, Riaan, Amy, - You have colored our lives with the paint of your love. We thank God for you all.

To our family (cousins, aunts and uncles) - Thank you for always loving us and welcoming us in your homes and lives. We love being back in South Africa and being able to see you guys again. Hendrik, thank you for always being more than a cousin to me, you are truly my older brother. The Steyn's, we love and appreciate you very much.

Our family at Eksderde - You guys are doing such valuable work! We love you. Andre and Zandia, we share a special bond with you...